STITCH & STENCIL
Over 25 Easy Fabric-Based Projects on
FLOWERS & FRUIT

This edition published by Silverdale Books,
an imprint of Bookmart Ltd, in 2000

Bookmart Ltd
Desford Road,
Enderby,
Leicester LE9 5AD

Registered Number 2372865

Produced by Eaglemoss Publications
Based on *Needlecraft Magic*
Copyright © Eaglemoss Publications Ltd 2000

Printed in Italy

ISBN 1-85605-590-6

10 9 8 7 6 5 4 3 2 1

CONTENTS

STOCKISTS AND SUPPLIERS

DMC cottons/floss:

DMC Creative World
Pullman Road
Wigston
Leicester LE18 2DY
UK

The DMC Corporation
Port Kearny
Building 10
South Kearny
New Jersey 07032
USA

DMC
51-66 Carrington Road
Marrickville
New South Wales 2204
Australia

Warnaar Trading Company Ltd
376 Ferry Road
PO Box 19567
Christchurch
New Zealand

S.A.T.C.
43 Somerset Road
PO Box 3868
Cape Town 8000
South Africa

Pebeo paints:

Pebeo UK
109 Solent Business Centre
Millbrook Road West
Millbrook
Southampton SO15 OHW
UK

Pebeo of America
Airport Road
PO Box 717
Swanton
VT 05488
USA

National Art Materials Pty Ltd
PO Box 678
Croydon
3136 Victoria
Australia

Pebeo Canada
1905 Roy Street
Sherbrooke
Quebec
Canada J1K 2X5

Lieserfam Investments Pty Ltd
PO Box 1721
Bedford View
2008 Johannesburg
South Africa

ACKNOWLEDGMENTS

Photographs: Paul Bricknell, Alan Duns, Christine Hanscombe, Gloria Nicol,
Lizzie Orme, Steven Pam, Lucinda Symons, Adrian Taylor, Shona Wood.

Illustrations: Terry Evans, Sally Holmes, Coral Mula.

Stencils by Tessa Brown.

POPPIES AND WHEAT

CRIMSON POPPIES DANCING IN GOLDEN WHEAT FIELDS
CAPTURE NATURE'S ART AND BOUNTY. USE YOUR
STENCILS TO CREATE MELLOW PICNIC LINENS, WITH
STITCHES ECHOING COUNTRYSIDE TEXTURES.

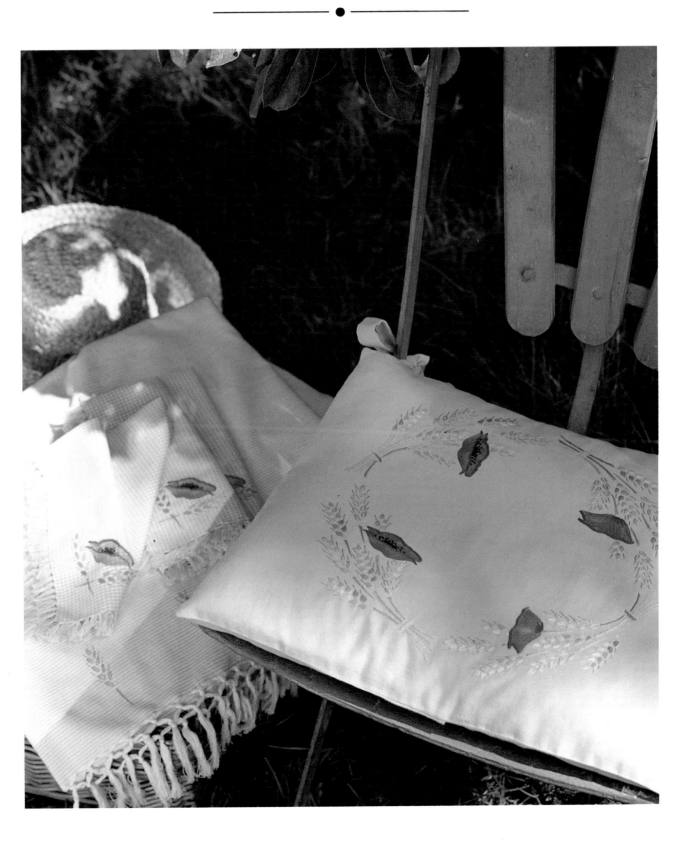

CUSHION WREATH

Picnic in comfort and style with this delightful chair cushion, or use it to give a country look to a conservatory, kitchen or dining room.

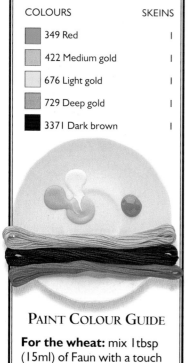

Stencil four sheaves of wheat head-to-tail to create this wreath. Both the open and furled poppies are set into the wreath and in order to stencil this, you need to mask off just a few stalks of the wheat. The diagram (top right) shows half the wreath and the sections that need to be masked off. It also shows the poppy cutouts. The poppies are made up of two stencils, one for the background and a second to add detail. The poppies are dry brushed in red paint to create a translucent effect. The petal outlines are given extra definition with a stencil overlay and a stem-stitch edging. The stamens on the open poppies are worked in satin stitch and French knots. Stencil and stitch the motifs before making up the cushion. For details on how to make easy cushion covers, refer to page 61.

Poppy A overlay

Poppy B

Poppy B overlay

Poppy A

Wheatsheaf B

Wheatsheaf A

Preparing to stencil

Fold the fabric square in half both ways, and finger press to mark the centre. Unfold the fabric. On each crease, measure and mark 5¾in (14.5cm) from the centre. Use these marks and the positioning diagram (left) to place the wheat sheaves. Before starting, mask off four and a half grains of wheat and section of stalk shaded red on sheaf A, and the poppy cutouts at base of sheaf. ◄

STENCILLING THE WREATH

1 Cover the work surface with paper and tape the fabric square right side up on top. Position the sheaf stencil at the top left, between the two creases, and stencil it in beige. Repeat to stencil sheaf at the bottom right.

2 Take the masking tape off the sheaf. Then mask off the five grains shaded red on sheaf B in the diagram above. Stencil the sheaf at the top right and then the bottom left of the fabric. ►

3 Position cutout of poppy A by top left sheaf. Dry brush in red paint. Reposition cutout and stencil motif by bottom left sheaf. Using cutout of poppy B, stencil motif by the top right sheaf and then the bottom right sheaf. Leave paint to dry. ◄

4 Use overlay of poppy A and red paint to outline poppy A at top left and then bottom left of fabric. Use overlay of poppy B to outline poppy B at top and then bottom right. Leave it to dry then set paint with a hot iron.

EMBROIDERING THE WREATH

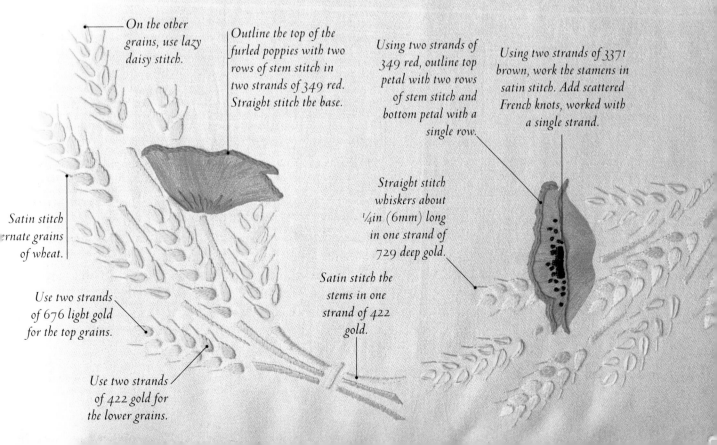

On the other grains, use lazy daisy stitch.

Outline the top of the furled poppies with two rows of stem stitch in two strands of 349 red. Straight stitch the base.

Using two strands of 349 red, outline top petal with two rows of stem stitch and bottom petal with a single row.

Using two strands of 3371 brown, work the stamens in satin stitch. Add scattered French knots, worked with a single strand.

Satin stitch [alt]ernate grains of wheat.

Straight stitch whiskers about ¼in (6mm) long in one strand of 729 deep gold.

Use two strands of 676 light gold for the top grains.

Satin stitch the stems in one strand of 422 gold.

Use two strands of 422 gold for the lower grains.

POPPY NAPKINS

Decorate ready-made napkins with an open poppy edged with interlacing stalks of wheat. Choose tassel-edged linens to echo fields of wheat swaying in the breeze.

YOU WILL NEED

❋ Napkins

❋ Stencil materials as listed for the cushion on page 6

❋ DMC stranded cottons/floss as listed in the colour key

❋ Embroidery needle, size 8

❋ Embroidery hoop

COLOUR KEY

COLOURS	SKEINS
349 Red	1
422 Medium gold	1
729 Deep gold	1
3371 Dark brown	1
3829 Golden brown	1

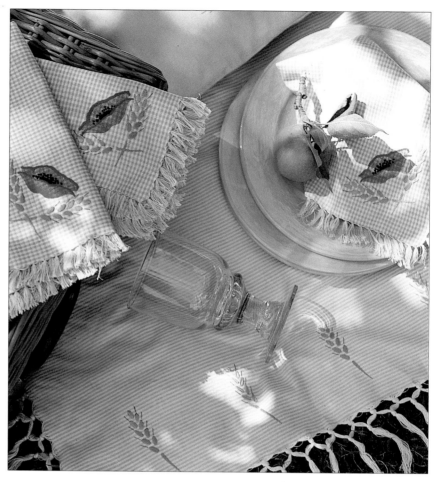

You can make a coordinating tablecloth by stencilling wheat stalks around the hem and embellishing them with simple embroidery.

Preparing the stencil

For the poppy napkins you need only the cutouts of a single stalk of wheat, poppy B and poppy B overlay. Before you start stencilling, mask off all the other cutouts.

STENCILLING THE MOTIFS

1 Fold the napkin in half diagonally, finger press, then unfold. Turn napkin 1½in (4cm) diagonally across one corner and finger press. Position wheat cutout with middle of stalk where the two folds cross and with the grains sloping to the left. Stencil motif in beige paint. Clean the stencil.

2 Flip over stencil and reposition cutout with stalk sloping to the right. Stencil in beige.

3 Position cutout of poppy B between the stalks and stencil in red. Leave to dry. Stencil over petal outlines with overlay B. When dry, set with a hot iron.

STITCHING THE MOTIFS

Using an embroidery hoop and two strands of cotton (floss), work the wheat grains in satin stitch – use 422 medium gold for the four top grains and 729 deep gold for the others. Satin stitch stems in 729. Use one strand of 3829 to straight stitch whiskers. Embroider the open poppy as shown on page 7.

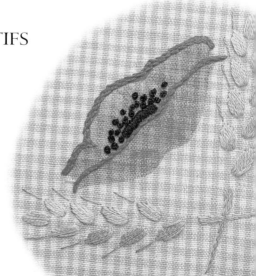

SUNFLOWERS

STENCILLED ONTO CITRUS FABRICS AND ENLIVENED
WITH EMBROIDERY AND BEADS, SUNFLOWERS GIVE A
CHEERY FEEL TO FURNISHINGS OR ACCESSORIES. PLANT
THE BLOOMS FREELY FOR YEAR-ROUND SUNSHINE.

SUNFLOWER TOTE BAG

Jazz up an everyday tote bag with a bold stencilled sunflower. Cross stitch and bead the flower centre for an eye-catching, textured effect.

YOU WILL NEED

* ❁ Cotton tote bag
* ❁ 4in (10cm) square of 10 mesh waste canvas
* ❁ Fabric paints in Havana Brown, Deep Brown, Gold Yellow and White
* ❁ Stencil and stencil brush
* ❁ White saucer
* ❁ Masking tape and card
* ❁ Wallpaper lining paper
* ❁ DMC stranded cotton/floss as listed in the colour key
* ❁ Embroidery needle, size 7
* ❁ Beading needle
* ❁ Air-soluble pen
* ❁ Packet of brown metallic seed beads
* ❁ Brown thread for sewing on the beads
* ❁ Tacking thread
* ❁ Tweezers

COLOUR KEY

COLOURS	SKEINS
■ 801 Brown	1

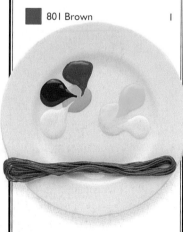

PAINT COLOUR GUIDE

For the deep yellow petals: mix Gold Yellow with a tiny dab of White.

For the pale yellow petals: mix Gold Yellow with a large dab of White.

For the brown centre: mix Havana Brown with a dash of Deep Brown and White.

The sunflower petals are stencilled in two layers using two shades of yellow to give depth to the motif. The first layer of petals is stencilled in deep yellow. The stencil cutout is then rotated slightly and the second layer of petals is stencilled in pale yellow. The centre of the flower is filled in by hand. The texture of the flower centre is suggested by large cross stitches, worked in stranded cotton (floss), using waste canvas. Brown metallic beads define the rim of the flower centre.

Preparing the stencil

The diagram (right) shows the complete sunflower stencil – the large sunflower petals cutout and the whole small sunflower cutout. For the tote bag you need only the cutout shown in colour – the large sunflower petals.

POSITIONING THE STENCIL

Using an air-soluble pen, mark the centre of the bag front with a small cross. Use the cross to help you position the petal cutout.

STENCILLING THE SUNFLOWER

1 Cover the work area with lining paper. Insert a piece of cardboard inside the bag to prevent paint seeping through to the back and tape the bag to the work top. Position the centre of the base of the petals cutout on the cross and stencil the upper sunflower petals in deep yellow. Turn the cutout through 180° and stencil in the lower petals. Leave to dry.

2 Re-position cutout on top half of motif and rotate it slightly so that the petal cutouts lie in between the painted petals. Using pale yellow, stencil a second layer of petals. Turn the cutout through 180° and stencil a second petal layer between the lower petals. ▼

3 Use the stencil brush and brown paint to colour in the centre of the flower. Leave the paint to dry. Remove protective cardboard, then set the paint with a hot iron. ▲

STITCHING THE SUNFLOWER

Using a contrasting coloured thread, tack the waste canvas over the sunflower head. Sewing through the canvas and the cotton fabric, work large cross stitches over the brown painted area using three strands of 801 brown. Leave a gap of two double threads between each cross and work the subsequent rows so they form a checkerboard effect. When the stitching is complete, remove tacking, dampen the canvas slightly and pull out the canvas threads with tweezers. Using a beading needle and brown sewing thread, sew the beads round the outer rim.

Use three strands of 801 brown to work the cross stitch.

Add a cluster of brown beads round the rim of the flower centre. Each one is sewn on separately.

FLORAL CURTAIN

Use the large sunflower cutout to brighten up a kitchen curtain or blind. Stencil the petals in yellow paint and cut the flower centres from fabric. Line up the blooms to form a border, arrange the flowers randomly or position them to fit in with the background pattern of your curtain.

YOU WILL NEED

❉ Curtain

❉ Stencilling equipment, as listed on page 10

❉ Small piece of cardboard

❉ Fabric remnants

❉ Scissors and pinking shears

❉ Pencil, ruler and compass

❉ Air-soluble fabric pen

❉ Pearl cotton in shade 666

❉ Embroidery needle, size 5

WORKING THE FLOWERS

1 Cover the work surface with lining paper and tape curtain on top. Decide where you want your blooms and then stencil on the petals in deep yellow, then pale yellow, as shown on page 11.

2 Using a compass and pencil, draw a 2¾in (7cm) diameter circle on to cardboard. Cut it out as a template.

3 Use an air-soluble marker to draw round the template onto your fabric remnants and use pinking shears to cut out the circles.

4 Tack each fabric circle in centre of the petals. Attach circles with 666 pearl cotton and running stitch worked ¼in (6mm) from the pinked edge. Remove the tacking.

Basic running stitch is all that is needed to attach the flower centres.

⊰ BRIGHT IDEAS ⊱

SUNNY TEA-TIME

Use the small sunflower cutout to decorate the corner of a napkin. Stencil the petals in deep and pale yellow and paint the flower centre in brown. Then sew French knots, worked with a double twist in two strands of DMC 300, round the outer rim of the flower centres.

SWEET PEAS

SWEET PEAS ADD A DELICATE TOUCH TO
BEDROOM LINENS. THEIR PRETTY PETALS AND
ELEGANT TENDRILS ARE SHOWN OFF TO
PERFECTION AGAINST WHITE.

SHEER DELIGHT

Single sweet pea florets on a sheer white curtain instil an air of romance. Suspend the curtain from a coronet above your bed, or hang it at the window, to sway gently in the breeze.

YOU WILL NEED

- ❀ White sheer curtain, washed and ironed
- ❀ Tape measure
- ❀ Fabric paints in White, Brilliant Green, Orange and Pink
- ❀ Stencil and stencil brushes
- ❀ Large white saucer
- ❀ Masking tape
- ❀ Wallpaper lining paper
- ❀ Kitchen paper
- ❀ Air-soluble fabric marker
- ❀ DMC stranded cottons/floss as listed in the colour key
- ❀ Embroidery needle, size 8
- ❀ Embroidery hoop

COLOUR KEY

COLOURS	SKEINS
604 Dark pink	1
605 Light pink	1
704 Bright green	1
3341 Dark orange	1
3824 Light orange	1

PAINT COLOUR GUIDE

For the stems: mix White with a small dab of Brilliant Green to make pale green.

For the flowers: mix White with a dab of Pink to make pale pink. Mix White with a dab of Orange to make peach.

The border is shown on the left-hand edge of the curtain, but you can place it anywhere you like to suit your bedroom – you can even repeat the design across the curtain for an allover pattern. The motifs are spaced 7in (18cm) apart at differing angles to imitate real-life sweet peas dangling from soft stems. If you like, you can flip the stencil occasionally to create a more varied pattern.

The florets are enhanced with fine stems and backstitched outlines. Straight stitches suggest shading on the open blooms, and the tightly furled buds are satin stitched.

Preparing the stencil
The diagram (left) shows the complete sweet peas stencil. For the curtain you need only the two florets shown in colour. You will be using their stems first, so before you start to stencil, mask off all the other cutouts.

Preparing the curtain
Fold the curtain lengthwise, 2¼in (6cm) from the left-hand edge, and press. Starting ¾in (2cm) above the bottom and working up, use the air-soluble fabric marker to mark the foldline at 7in (18cm) intervals.

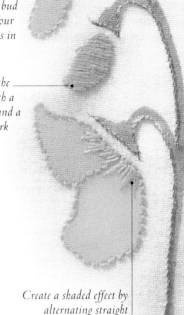

Use two strands of light orange to outline the top bud and to work four straight stitches in the centre.

Satin stitch the lower bud with a strand of pale and a strand of dark orange.

Create a shaded effect by alternating straight stitches of dark orange with light orange.

STENCILLING THE CURTAIN

1 Prepare the work surface, lay the curtain out flat across it and tape it in place. Position the stencil just above the foldline, with the base of the lower flower stem level with the first mark. Stencil the stem in pale green. Clean and dry the stencil.

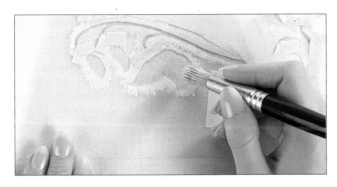

2 Reposition the stencil so that the base of the stem on the second floret is level with the second mark; if you like, tilt it slightly. Stencil the stem in pale green. Continue in this way to stencil the two stems alternately along the curtain. ▲

3 Unmask the flowers and buds. Mask off the stems, leaving a small section showing to help position the stencil. Using peach, stencil the flowers and buds on alternate florets. Clean the brush and stencil; stencil remaining flowers in pale pink. When dry, set the paints according to manufacturer's instructions. ▲

Satin stitch this bud in two strands of dark pink.

Fill the smallest bud with satin stitches, worked in two strands of light pink.

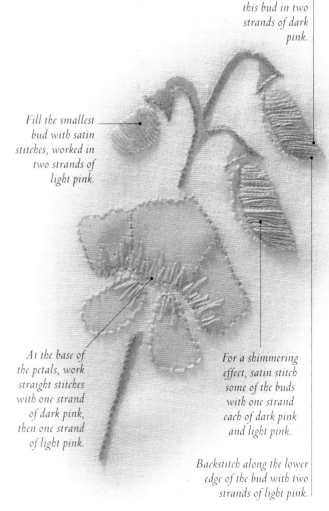

STITCHING THE CURTAIN

Use one strand of bright green to stem stitch one side of the stems. Use two strands of dark pink to backstitch around the large petal of the open pink flower and light pink for the small petals. Define the base of the petals with straight stitches worked in two different colours.

Outline the half-open flower in two strands of dark orange and work the straight stitches with one strand of dark orange, then light orange. To outline and fill in the buds, refer to the stitch details (right).

At the base of the petals, work straight stitches with one strand of dark pink, then one strand of light pink.

For a shimmering effect, satin stitch some of the buds with one strand each of dark pink and light pink.

Backstitch along the lower edge of the bud with two strands of light pink.

Sweet Pea Pillowcase

You Will Need

❋ White pillowcase, washed and ironed

❋ Stiff cardboard, 20in (50cm) square

❋ Spray mount

❋ Black waterproof (permanent) marker

❋ Stencilling materials, as listed on page 14

❋ Fabric paints as listed on page 14, plus Veridian

❋ Tracing paper, ruler and sharp pencil

❋ Dressmaker's carbon paper

❋ Wallpaper lining paper

❋ DMC stranded cottons/floss as listed in the colour key

❋ Embroidery needle, size 8

❋ Embroidery hoop

Colour Key

COLOURS		SKEINS
	368 Mid green	I
	504 Pale green	I
	604 Dark pink	I
	605 Light pink	I
	704 Bright green	I
	3341 Dark orange	I
	3824 Light orange	I

Paint Colour Guide

For the leaves and stems: make pale green as shown on page 14. Mix White with a dab of Veridian to make pale veridian.

For the flowers: mix pale pink and peach as on page 14.

The sweet pea pillowcase shows how you can repeat the whole stencil design to make a flowing border, reminiscent of sweet peas climbing a fence. The tendrils are added after the design has been stencilled, using the trace-off diagrams below right.

Preparing the stencil

You will need the complete stencil for the pillowcase. To help you position the stencil, use a pencil and ruler to draw a line down the centre of the design. You will be using the leaves and stalks first, so before you start, mask off all the flowers and buds.

Preparing the pillowcase

On the cardboard, mark a line 6in (15cm) from one edge with the black waterproof marker. Slide the cardboard into the pillowcase so that the black line shows through the fabric, 6in (15cm) from the closed end. The cardboard will also prevent the paint seeping through to the back.

STENCILLING THE PILLOWCASE

1 Cover the work surface with wallpaper lining paper and tape the pillowcase on top. Mask off the lower pair of leaves on the stencil. Spray mount the back and allow it to dry. Position the centre line on the stencil over the guideline on the cardboard, with the base of the main stem on the base of the pillowcase.

2 Using pale green, stencil the leaves and stems, applying the paint unevenly. With the second brush and pale veridian, go over the leaves and stalks again to create a broken, patchy effect. Unmask the lower leaves. ◄

3 Position the stencil with the base of the main stem just above the top of the first stem. Match the centre line of the stencil to the drawn line and stencil the leaves and stems in two colours as before. Remove the masking tape. Clean and dry the stencil and brushes. ►

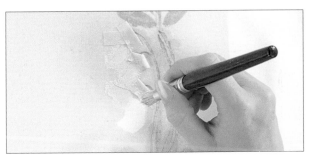

4 Mask off all stems that are near the flowers and buds. Position the stencil over the lower set of stems and leaves, and stencil one group of flowers and buds in peach and one in pale pink. Repeat to stencil the second group of flowers and buds. ▲

STITCHING THE PILLOWCASE

Trace tendrils (below) and transfer them to the design with dressmaker's carbon paper. Mount the stencilled layer of fabric in the hoop. Stitch the flowers, buds and flower stems in the same way as curtain. Refer to stitch details (right) to embroider stems, leaves and tendrils.

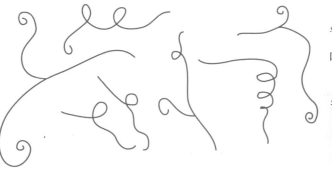

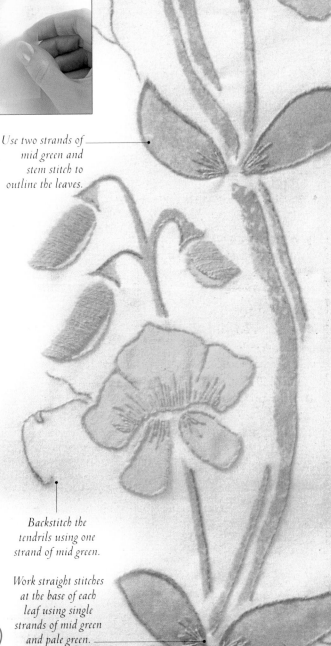

Outline one edge of the flower stems in stem stitch, using one strand of bright green.

Stem stitch one side of the main stems using one strand of mid green.

Use two strands of mid green and stem stitch to outline the leaves.

Backstitch the tendrils using one strand of mid green.

Work straight stitches at the base of each leaf using single strands of mid green and pale green.

DUVET COVER

Complete your bedroom set with a duvet cover, stencilled with trails of sweet peas to create an allover design. The instructions here explain how to stencil a single duvet cover.

Backstitch the tendrils with a single strand of mid green.

Stencilling the duvet

Fold the duvet cover in half lengthwise, then fold it in half lengthwise again. Press it to make three vertical fold-lines. Stencil a continuous border down each foldline, as shown for the pillowcase on the previous page.

Adding the tendrils

Mark the tendrils as given for the pillowcase. If you wish, embroider the cover to match the pillowcase but, as shown here, it looks just as good with just the tendrils worked in backstitch with one strand of mid green.

SWEET PEA SACHET

A single spray of sweet peas is a pretty decoration for scented sachets. Cut two 8 x 6in (20 x 15cm) rectangles of fabric. Stencil a spray of sweet peas in the centre of one rectangle and embroider the motif. Stitch the fabric pieces right sides together, leaving an opening in one edge. Turn it out, fill it with potpourri and slipstitch closed. Add a matching ribbon, secured with French knots.

BRIGHT IDEAS

PRETTY KEEPSAKE

When stencilling the curtain, stencil an extra sweet pea floret onto a square of fabric and turn it into a small bag that is perfect for keeping treasured items. Embroider the motif, then right sides together, stitch the sides and base. Turn in a narrow hem at the top and secure it with French knots. Tie the top with fine ribbon.

PEAR PERFECT

WITH THEIR REALISTICALLY MOTTLED SKIN,
THESE PLUMP, PERFECTLY FORMED PEARS
BRING THE FRESHNESS OF COUNTRY
ORCHARDS TO THE KITCHEN.

KITCHEN LINENS

Set on creamy calico/muslin patches and blanket stitched onto an apron and tablecloth, these pears look good as a paint effect, or given extra form with cross-hatched stitches.

YOU WILL NEED

❋ Apron

❋ 3⅞yd (3.5m) green cotton fabric, 52in (130cm) wide

❋ Matching sewing thread

❋ ⅝yd (50cm) lightweight unbleached calico/muslin, 50in (127cm) wide

❋ Fabric paints in Spring Green, Havana Brown and White

❋ Stencil and two stencil brushes

❋ Masking tape

❋ Wallpaper lining paper

❋ Kitchen paper

❋ DMC stranded cotton/floss as listed in the colour key

❋ Embroidery needle, size 8

❋ Embroidery hoop

COLOUR KEY

COLOURS	SKEINS
987 Green	2

PAINT COLOUR GUIDE

To make pale green: mix a dab of White into one third of a pot of Spring Green.

To make pale brown: mix a dab of White into 1 tbsp (15ml) of Havana Brown.

The pears are stencilled in pale green and Spring Green, with pale brown shading down one side to give them a plump, rounded look. Each new layer of fabric paint is applied while the previous layer is still wet, so that the colours blend together to imitate the mottled look so typical of real-life pears.

The apron is embellished with two pear patches which face in opposite directions for a balanced look. Long straight stitches, worked in green cotton (floss), give a cross-hatched effect. The patches are then blanket stitched to the apron using the same colour cotton (floss).

The tablecloth is decorated with four patches on each side. The pears have been left as a paint effect here, but you could embroider them to match the apron, if you wish. The finished tablecloth is 65in (1.65m) square. To make a smaller or larger tablecloth, just adjust the number of patches accordingly.

Preparing the stencil

The diagram (below) shows the complete pear stencil. The whole design is used each time.

Preparing the fabric

Wash the calico (muslin) to pre-shrink it. Press the fabric, then cut two 8 x 6in (20 x 15cm) rectangular patches for the apron, and 16 for the tablecloth.

STENCILLING THE PEARS

1 Protect the work surface with lining paper, and tape a calico (muslin) square on top. Centre the pear cutout on the calico (muslin) with the pear tilted at a slight angle. Stencil in pale green paint, then quickly dab on a little Spring Green to create a mottled effect. ◄

2 While the green paint is still wet, use the second brush to dab on a little pale brown paint down one side to create a shaded effect. Stencil eight more patches with the pear facing in the same direction. Clean and dry the stencil and brush. ▶

3 Flip the stencil so the pear faces the other way. Stencil the remaining nine patches, following steps 2-3. Set all the paints with a hot iron.

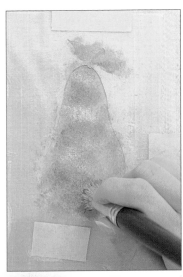

STITCHING THE APRON

Mount a stencilled patch in the hoop. Use two strands of green cotton (floss) to embroider the pear; refer to the stitch details (right). Embroider a second pear facing in the opposite direction.

Turn in and press the raw edges of each patch, so they measure 6 x 4in (15 x 10cm). Trim away the excess fabric. Pin the patches onto the apron and secure with blanket stitch, using two strands of embroidery cotton (floss).

MAKING THE TABLECLOTH

Cut two 68 x 34⅜in (173 x 87.5cm) rectangles of green fabric. Stitch them right sides together down one long edge, taking a ⅜in (1cm) seam. Press the seam open.

Press a ¾in (2cm) double hem all around the cloth, folding the corners into neat mitres. Machine stitch the hem in place.

Stitch 16 patches onto the tablecloth, as for the apron (above). Place four on each side, with the pears facing in alternate directions. Place the first one 15¾in (40cm) from one end and 2¾in (7cm) above the hem. Space remaining patches 6in (15cm) apart and the same distance from the hem.

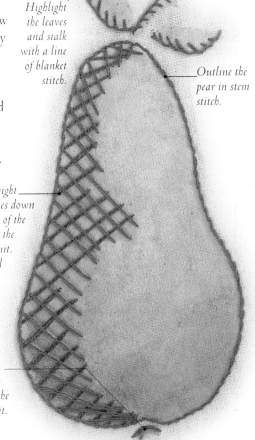

Highlight the leaves and stalk with a line of blanket stitch.

Outline the pear in stem stitch.

Work long straight diagonal stitches down the shaded side of the pear to suggest the curve of the fruit. Make diagonal stitches in the opposite direction to create a cross-hatched effect.

Single straight stitches suggest the dimple at the base of the fruit.

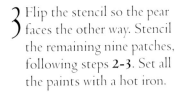

FRAMED PEAR PICTURE

The pear is stencilled onto lustrous Dupion silk furnishing fabric, using gold paint and metallic gold thread to give the fruit a realistic sheen. Gold and several different green threads are used to create the shading for a subtle painterly effect. Choose a mount and frame to complement both the finished picture and the room.

YOU WILL NEED

❋ Cream Dupion silk furnishing fabric, 11 x 9½in (28 x 24cm)
❋ Fabric paints and stencilling equipment as listed on page 20
❋ Fabric paint in Gold
❋ DMC stranded cottons/floss as listed in the colour key
❋ Embroidery needle, size 8
❋ Embroidery hoop

COLOUR KEY

COLOURS	SKEINS
471 Light green	1
987 Dark green	1
3347 Mid green	1
5258 Metallic gold	1

STENCILLING THE DESIGN

Keep the brushes very dry to prevent the paint bleeding into the uneven grain of the silk. Mix the paints and stencil the pear onto the silk, as on pages 20-21. Leave the stencil in place and, when the paint is dry, dab on a little gold paint. ➤

STITCHING THE PEAR

Use a single strand of cotton (floss) throughout. Referring to page 21, cross hatch both sides of the pear. On the dark side, use dark green first, then work stitches in the opposite direction in mid green. On the light side, use light green, then gold. Refer to the details below to outline the pear and shade the leaves.

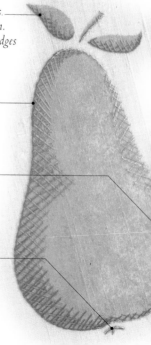

Cross-hatch the leaves in dark and mid green. Stemstitch the lower edges in dark green.

Outline the dark side in stem stitch using dark green.

Taper the gold diagonal stitches off towards the bottom of the pear.

Stem stitch the base of the pear, using dark green, then gold.

SUMMER DAISIES

SUMMERY SKY BLUE, GRASS GREEN, BRIGHT
SUNSHINE YELLOW AND CRISP WHITE COMBINE
TO BRING A DAISY-FRESH LOOK TO A TRIO
OF BEDROOM ACCESSORIES.

PATCHWORK DAISY QUILT

Combine the arts of stencilling, patchwork and machine quilting to create a cheerful bed cover. Its sunny colours and informal look will brighten up your bedroom.

YOU WILL NEED

- ❋ 3¼yd (3m) of 44in (112cm) wide blue cotton fabric
- ❋ 1⅛yd (1m) of 44in (112cm) wide green cotton fabric
- ❋ ¾yd (70cm) of 56in (142cm) wide yellow checked fabric
- ❋ Lightweight polyester wadding/batting, (65½ x 49½in (164 x 124cm)
- ❋ 2¾yd (2.5m) of 44in (112cm) wide white cotton lawn or muslin backing fabric
- ❋ 8¾in (22cm) square cardboard template
- ❋ Fabric paints in White and Buttercup
- ❋ Stencil and stencil brush
- ❋ Large saucer
- ❋ Kitchen paper and wallpaper lining paper
- ❋ Masking tape
- ❋ Tacking thread and needle
- ❋ White and clear nylon sewing threads

PAINT COLOUR GUIDE

For the flower centres: mix Buttercup with White to make bright yellow.

Green fabric patches, stencilled with white daisies, are alternated with yellow checked patches and framed with sky blue block borders. Contour quilting, machine stitched with clear nylon sewing thread, adds subtle surface texture to the design.

The finished patchwork quilt measures 64 x 48in (160 x 120cm) – the perfect size for a cot or lap quilt. If you want to make it larger, simply add extra squares and cut longer border strips. Remember to wash and iron all your fabrics before cutting them out and stencilling them – for speed and accuracy, use the cardboard template to cut out the patches. Take ⅜in (1cm) seam allowances throughout, and press and trim the seams carefully.

Preparing the stencil

The diagram (right) shows the complete stencil. For the quilt, you need the flower centre, the large daisy petals and the central alignment hole. The petals are stencilled first, so mask off the other cutouts.

Cutting out

From green fabric: use the template to cut 18 squares.
From yellow checked fabric: use the template to cut 17 squares.
From blue fabric: for the borders, cut two 56¾ x 4¾in (142 x 12cm) strips and two 48¾ x 4¾in (122 x 12cm) strips. For the quilt back, cut two 48¾ x 32¾in (122 x 82cm) rectangles.
From white fabric: cut two 48¾ x 32¾in (122 x 82cm) rectangles for the backing.

MAKING UP THE QUILT

Lay out the squares right side up as shown above. Pin and stitch them in horizontal strips, then join the strips. Add the blue border strips in pairs to opposite sides, longer edges first.

Join two long edges of the white fabric rectangles. Sandwich the wadding (batting) between the quilt top and the white fabric; tack. With clear nylon thread, machine quilt the daisies, working around the petals and centre in one movement. Machine quilt between the patches, pulling the fabrics flat as you stitch.

For the quilt back, join two long edges of the blue rectangles. Right sides together, stitch to the quilted top, leaving an 8in (20cm) gap in one seam. Turn through to the right side. Slipstitch the opening closed. With the quilt top facing up, machine quilt along the inner edge of the blue border.

STENCILLING THE DAISIES

1 Fold the green patches in half both ways and finger press – the creases cross at the centre. Position the petal cutout with the central alignment hole over the centre of the patch. Stencil the upper half of the petals in white. Stencil each green square in this way.

2 Reposition the stencil, centring the alignment hole as before, and stencil the lower petals on each flower. Take off the masking tape. Clean and dry the stencil and brush. ►

3 Position the flower centre cutout between the petals, and stencil in bright yellow. Leave the fabric paints to dry, then set them with a hot iron. ◄

Machine quilt in a continuous flow, stitching the centre of the flower at the base of each petal as you work.

DRAWSTRING BAG

The drawstring bag has two useful patch pockets decorated with small daisies. The daisies are satin stitched in white, green and yellow, with the stems done in stem stitch. The pockets are embroidered, then folded double and stitched in place before the bag is made up.

Stencilling the daisies first in white gives you a useful stitching guide, but you can simply mark the fabric by drawing around the inside of the daisy cutouts. The bag measures 11½ x 8in (29 x 20cm). Take ⅝in (1.5cm) seams throughout.

YOU WILL NEED

* ½yd (40cm) of 44in (112cm) wide blue cotton fabric
* Green cotton fabric, 12in (30cm) square
* Fabric paint in White
* Stencilling equipment as listed on page 24
* Air-soluble fabric marker
* Embroidery hoop
* DMC stranded cottons/floss as listed in the colour key
* Embroidery needle, size 9
* Blue sewing thread

COLOUR KEY

COLOURS	SKEINS
White	1
743 Yellow	1
913 Green	1

Preparing the stencil

The diagram (left) shows the complete daisy stencil. For the pocket design, you need the small daisy and leaf cutouts.

Cutting out

From blue fabric: cut two 16⅛ x 9¼in (40 x 23cm) rectangles for the bag. For the drawstring, cut a 2¾in (7cm) wide strip across the full width of the fabric.

From green fabric: cut a 10¾ x 9¼in (27 x 23cm) pocket rectangle.

Positioning the design

Fold the green fabric in half lengthwise, wrong sides together, and press. Fold in half again widthwise and finger press. Unfold just the finger-pressed fold. With the air-soluble fabric marker, make dots 2in (5cm) to each side of the finger-pressed fold, placing them 1¾in (4.5cm) below the pressed fold. From the dots, draw 2⅛in (5.5cm) long vertical lines towards the lower raw edges. Unfold the fabric.

STENCILLING THE POCKET

Centre the flower centre over one of the dots and stencil the flower centre, petals and leaves in white. Repeat to stencil another daisy at the second marked dot. Leave the paint to dry, then set it with a hot iron, following the manufacturer's instructions. ➤

STITCHING THE BAG

Mount the stencilled fabric in the embroidery hoop. Use two strands of cotton (floss) throughout and refer to the stitch details below. Satin stitch the petals in white cotton (floss). Using yellow, work the centres in padded satin stitch. Using green, satin stitch the leaves and work the stems in stem stitch.

Refold the pocket along the pressed line. Raw edges matching, tack the pocket to the base of one blue fabric rectangle. Using blue thread, machine stitch along the vertical foldline. Make up the bag with the casing set below the top. Thread a strip of fabric through the casing for the drawstring.

Satin stitch the petals in white, starting at the centre of each petal and working outwards.

Fill the centre of the daisies with padded satin stitch using yellow.

Satin stitch the leaves in green. Work two bands, slanting the stitches inwards to the centre of each leaf to create a veined effect.

Embroider the stalks in stem stitch using green. Stitch along the vertical lines made with the fabric marker.

DAISY CUSHION

This patchwork cushion cover combines machine and hand quilting. The large daisy is hand quilted with yellow cotton (floss), and clear nylon thread is used to machine quilt around the edges of the border. Yellow buttons highlight the centres of the small corner daisies. Mix the paint as shown on page 24.

The finished daisy cushion measures 15¾in (40cm) square. Take ⅜in (1cm) seam allowances throughout.

YOU WILL NEED

❋ ½yd (40cm) of 44in (112cm) wide blue cotton fabric

❋ ⅛yd (10cm) of 44in (112cm) wide green cotton fabric

❋ ⅛yd (10cm) of 56in (143cm) wide yellow check fabric

❋ White cotton backing fabric, 16in (40cm) square

❋ Lightweight polyester wadding/batting, 16in (40cm) square

❋ Fabric paints and stencilling equipment as listed on page 24

❋ Tacking thread and needle

❋ One skein of DMC stranded cotton/floss, 743 yellow

❋ Clear nylon sewing thread

❋ Large embroidery hoop

❋ Embroidery needle, size 8

❋ Four yellow buttons, ½in (1.2cm) diameter

❋ Cushion pad, 15¾in (40cm) square

CUTTING AND STENCILLING

1 *From blue fabric:* cut one 9½in (24cm) square and four 4in (10cm) squares. For the cushion cover back, cut two 16¾ x 12in (42 x 30cm) rectangles. *From green fabric:* cut two 9½ x 1⅛in (24 x 3cm) strips and two 10¼ x 1⅛in (26 x 3cm) strips. *From yellow fabric:* cut four 10¼ x 4in (26 x 10cm) rectangles.

2 Fold the large blue square in quarters and finger press the folds. Stencil a large daisy in the centre, as shown on page 25, steps **1-3**.

3 Mask off the centre and leaves of the small daisy. Stencil the petals in white on each of the four small blue squares. ▲

MAKING THE CUSHION COVER

Following the diagram (right), assemble the front of the cushion cover, taking ⅜in (1cm) seams. Sandwich the wadding (batting) between the patchwork and the white backing and tack together. With three strands of yellow cotton (floss), hand quilt around the petals and the centre of the large daisy. Using clear nylon thread, machine quilt around the edges of the border. Stitch a button to the centre of each small daisy. Make up the cushion cover as on page 61.

LEMON AND LIME

THE SHARP COLOURS OF CITRUS FRUIT, OFFSET
BY ACID PINK, MAKE A SIZZLING SETTING FOR
COOLING DRINKS TO QUENCH
A SUMMER THIRST.

CITRUS TRAY CLOTH

Lemon slices and a whole lemon, stencilled
onto brilliant green, are brought to life with
textured embroidery stitches.

YOU WILL NEED

* Two rectangles of bright green cotton fabric the size of your tray
* Bright pink cotton fabric and matching sewing thread for the binding
* Fabric paints in Buttercup, Lemon Yellow and Light Green
* Stencil and stencil brush
* Large white saucer
* Kitchen paper and wallpaper lining paper
* Masking tape
* DMC stranded cottons/floss as listed in the colour key
* Embroidery needle, size 9

COLOUR KEY

COLOURS	SKEINS
444 Dark yellow	I
702 Dark green	I
727 Pale yellow	I

PAINT COLOUR GUIDE

To make bright yellow: mix equal quantities of Buttercup and Lemon Yellow.

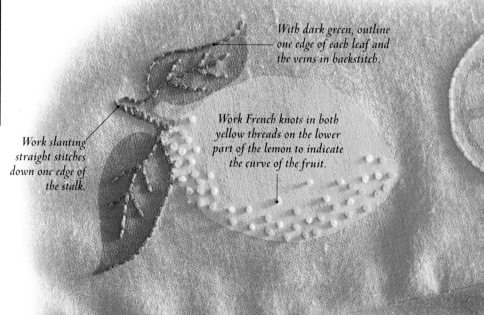

With dark green, outline one edge of each leaf and the veins in backstitch.

Work slanting straight stitches down one edge of the stalk.

Work French knots in both yellow threads on the lower part of the lemon to indicate the curve of the fruit.

This sizzling citrus tray cloth shows how you can use the same stencil motifs in different ways to create unique designs. Three of the images are created from just one cutout – the full lemon slice, the half slice and the quarter slice.

With such a simple design you can use really strong, bold colours. A bright yellow lemon and lemon slices are stencilled onto acid green fabric. Embroidery stitches add texture, and suggest the peel and pips on the lemon slices. Hot pink bias binding makes a bold edging for the cloth.

Preparing the fabric

Fold one green fabric rectangle lengthwise, 1¼in (3cm) from the bottom edge, and finger press. Then fold it widthwise, 1¼in (3cm) from the left-hand edge, and finger press. Use the foldlines as a guide for positioning the design.

Preparing the stencil

The diagram (below) shows the complete citrus stencil. For the tray cloth you need the whole lemon, the stalk and leaf and the citrus slice, shown here in colour. Mask off any cutouts you don't need close to the cutout you are using.

STENCILLING THE TRAY CLOTH

1 Position the leaf and stalk cutout at an angle, with the tip of the lower leaf in the corner made by the foldlines. Stencil with light green fabric paint. Clean and dry the stencil and brush.

2 Position the whole lemon cutout close to the end of the stalk. Angle it slightly so that the lower edge of the lemon rests on the finger-pressed crease. Stencil in bright yellow paint. ➤

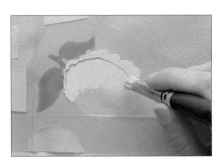

3 For the whole lemon slice, place the half-slice cutout on the foldline, ¾in (2cm) to the right of the lemon. Stencil it in bright yellow. Rotate the cutout and stencil the second half. ▼

4 Angle the half-slice lemon cutout on the foldline, ¾in (2cm) from the whole slice. Stencil it in bright yellow. Mask off half the slice cutout to make a quarter slice. Stencil it on the foldline, ¾in (2cm) from the half slice. When the paints are dry, set them with an iron. ➤

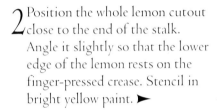

STITCHING THE FRUIT

Use three strands of cotton (floss) in the needle to backstitch outlines around the slices, work the pips and add details to the leaf, stalk and the whole lemon.

With dark yellow, backstitch around the slices.

Assembling the tray cloth

Pin the two fabric rectangles wrong sides together, raw edges matching. Round off the corners with scissors.

From the pink fabric: make ¾in (2cm) wide bias binding. Use it to bind the edges of the tray cloth.

*zy daisy stitches
e yellow to
te the pips.*

LEMON AND LIME COASTERS

Backstitch the outline of the leaves, veins and slice in dark green.

Stitch French knots in pale green and mid green on the lime. Use pale green and lazy stitch to work the pips in the lime slice.

Vary the citrus fruit theme with a set of lemon and lime coasters to perk up your drinks tray. Make a set of four, with two to match the tray cloth, and switch the colours for the other two, by stencilling green citrus fruits onto yellow fabric. Bind all four with hot pink bias binding.

For the set, you will need four 5½in (14cm) yellow fabric squares and four 5½in (14cm) bright green fabric squares, plus the pink fabric and the stencilling equipment and paints listed on page 30. Each coaster measures 5½in (14cm) square.

COLOUR KEY	
COLOURS	SKEINS
444 Dark yellow	1
472 Pale green	1
702 Dark green	1
704 Mid green	1
727 Pale yellow	1

STENCILLING THE COASTERS

1 Stencil the whole lime in light green on a yellow fabric square, about ¾in (2cm) from one corner. Add the stalk and leaves in light green. As in step **3** on page 31, use light green to stencil a lime slice on another yellow square.

2 On one green square, use bright yellow to stencil a whole lemon slice. On another green square, use bright yellow to stencil a whole lemon.

STITCHING THE COASTERS

Use three strands of cotton (floss) throughout. Embroider the lemon and the lemon slice as shown on the previous page, using the same cotton (floss) colours.

Use the same stitches for the lime and lime slice, referring to the stitch details (above) for cotton (floss) colours.

To make up the coasters, pin each embroidered square to a matching plain square, wrong sides together. Bind the edges with pink bias binding.

BRIGHT IDEAS

CITRUS TEATOWEL

Decorate a teatowel with a mixture of whole, half and quarter lime slices. Use light green to stencil the slices close to one corner, and stitch them in the same way as the coasters and tray cloth.

VASES OF FLOWERS

MARK THE SEASONAL CHANGES WITH
TWO VASES OF FLOWERS, STENCILLED
AND STITCHED IN AUTUMN OR SPRING
COLOURS ON A CUSHION AND TIEBACK.

AUTUMN CUSHION

Three different flowers in rich russets and golden browns are teamed with stalks of wheat to make a mellow autumnal arrangement.

YOU WILL NEED

* ⅝yd (50cm) of 48in (120cm) wide beige furnishing fabric
* 1⅞yd (1.70m) dark blue piping
* Fabric paints in France Blue, Vermilion, Havana Brown and White
* Large white saucer
* Flower and vase stencil
* Poppies and wheat stencil (page 75)
* Stencil brush
* Masking tape
* Kitchen paper and wallpaper lining paper
* Spray mount
* Sharp pencil
* DMC stranded cottons/floss as listed in the colour key
* Embroidery needle, size 9
* Embroidery hoop
* Cushion pad, 15in (38cm) square

COLOUR KEY

COLOURS	SKEINS
300 Dark brown	1
400 Mid brown	1
676 Light gold	1
729 Dark gold	1
919 Dark burnt orange	1
921 Burnt orange	1
945 Pearl pink	1

PAINT COLOUR GUIDE

For the background flowers: mix White with a tiny dab of Vermilion and Havana Brown to make pale salmon pink.

For the foreground flowers: mix Havana Brown with a dab of Vermilion and White to make mid brown. Mix Vermilion with a dab of Havana Brown and White to make mid red.

For the wheat: mix White with a dab of Havana Brown to make light brown.

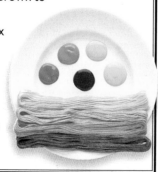

The background flowers are stencilled first in a pale colour, and the foreground blooms are stencilled on top in richer shades, with stalks of wheat from the poppies and wheat stencil on page 75. The blue and white vase is stencilled last. The flowers are enlivened with embroidery worked in rich colours and a variety of stitches. The cushion cover is finished with a smart blue piped trim to echo the colour of the vase. The finished cushion cover measures 15in (38cm) square.

Preparing the stencils

The diagram (top right) shows the complete flower and vase stencil. To create the autumn cushion you will need all the cutouts except the leaf sprig. When you are stencilling, mask off any cutouts near the one you are using.

The diagram (bottom right) shows the poppies and wheat stencil, from pages 5–8. Choose any one of the cutouts and mask off any cutouts near it.

Preparing the fabric

Cut a piece of fabric 16in (41cm) square for the cushion front. Fold it in half both ways and finger press to mark the centre. Centre the vase cutout on the vertical crease with the top of the vase 1in (2.5cm) below the centre of the fabric. Mark its position with small pencil marks around the outline. Use the marks to position the vase cutout.

STENCILLING THE DESIGN

1 Using pale salmon pink paint and following the positioning diagram (right), stencil six background flowers. Clean and dry the stencil and brush, and allow the paint to dry.

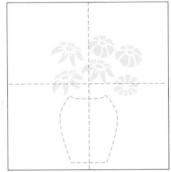

2 Following the positioning diagram (right), stencil the foreground flowers in mid brown and mid red paint. Clean and dry the stencil and brush. ➤

3 Using the poppies and wheat stencil, and light brown paint, stencil stalks of wheat randomly around the arrangement. Leave the paints to dry.

4 Use small pieces of masking tape to cover any stencilled petals that overlap the marked position of the vase. Spray mount the back of the vase cutout and allow to dry.

5 Realign the vase cutout, using the pencil marks as a guide, and stencil the vase in France Blue. Allow the paint to dry. Set all the paints with a hot iron.

STITCHING THE AUTUMN CUSHION

Two strands of embroidery thread (floss) are used throughout. Start by outlining the background flowers in backstitch using 945 pearl pink.

Work the foreground flowers in a mixture of satin, long and short, stem and straight stitch, with French knots filling some of the centres. Use 300 dark brown and 400 mid brown for flowers stencilled in mid brown paint, and 919 dark burnt orange and 921 burnt orange for flowers stencilled in mid red. Work the stitches in the directions shown in the photograph and refer to the details below for stitching instructions.

Work satin stitch from the widest part of the petal outwards to give the petals a rounded effect.

Fill the centres with French knots.

Use straight stitches for the whisker

Satin stitch the lower grains and stalks in dark gold. Work each grain from the base to the tip.

Work the large petals in long and short stitch, blending in a darker shade at the base of the petals.

Outline the background flowers in backstitch and pearl pink.

Outline the petals with stem stitch, and work straight stitches at the base of each in a lighter shade.

Using light gold, work two lazy daisy stitches, one inside the other, for the upper grains.

Making up the cushion

Make up the cushion cover, using the stencilled fabric for the front, and taking ⅝in (1.5cm) seams, as on page 61. For the piping, stitch it in place on the right side of the fabric, matching up the raw edges. Ease round the corners, clipping into the seam allowances and overlap by 1in (2.5cm). Trim the cord (but not the fabric), fold under ⅜in (1cm) of the overlapping fabric end, lap it over the other end, and stitch in place.

CURTAIN TIEBACK

This lightly embroidered tieback coordinates perfectly with the autumn cushion. If you prefer, you can stitch the flowers to match the cushion, as shown left.

For the tieback, use one of the special tieback kits which contain full instructions and a pattern, and make up the tieback in the same fabric and piping as the cushion. You will need dark blue piping, ⅜yd (30cm) of fabric, and the embroidery threads and stencilling equipment listed on page 34. You will also need all the fabric paints listed except France Blue.

Work backstitch around the petals and satin stitch the centre.

Preparing the stencils

The diagram (left) shows the complete stencil. For the tieback, you will need the three blooms, shown in colour. You will also need one of the stalks of wheat from the poppies and wheat stencil, as shown on page 35.

Outline the petals with stem stitch and work straight stitches at the bases in a lighter shade.

Work running stitch around the petals and straight stitches at the base of each. Fill the centre with French knots.

WORKING THE DESIGN

1 Use the pattern piece provided with the kit to draw the shape of the tieback onto the fabric. Mark the centre line with a finger-pressed crease. Mark the stitching line with a pencil. Stencil all the motifs within the stitching line. ▶

2 Stencil a mid brown flower on the centre crease. Stencil a light brown stalk on either side, then a mid red flower. Continue to stencil alternate flowers and stalks, working out from the centre in both directions. ◀

3 Refer to page 36 to embroider the wheat. Work the flowers as shown above, referring to page 36 for cotton (floss) colours. Use straight stitches at the base of some petals and fill the centres with French knots or satin stitch.

SPRING CUSHION

YOU WILL NEED

- ⁵⁄₈yd (50cm) of 48in (120cm) wide cream furnishing fabric
- 1⁷⁄₈yd (1.70m) dark blue piping
- Fabric paints in France Blue, Brilliant Green, Orange, Pink and White
- Stencilling equipment as listed on page 34
- DMC stranded cottons/floss as listed in the colour key
- Embroidery needle, size 9
- Embroidery hoop
- Cushion pad, 15in (38cm) square

COLOUR KEY

COLOURS	SKEINS
957 Pink	1
992 Green	1
3326 Light pink	1
3340 Orange	1
3341 Light orange	1

PAINT COLOUR GUIDE

For the background flowers: mix White with a dab of Orange and Pink to make pale peach.

For the foreground flowers: mix Pink with White to make mid pink, and Orange with White to make mid orange.

For the leaves: mix White with a dab of Brilliant Green to make pale green.

The flower arrangement takes on a different look with brighter colours stencilled and stitched on cream silky fabric. Fresh green leaves replace the stalks of wheat for a lively spring-like feel, and the design is embellished with just a few simple stitches. Pipe the cushion in dark blue as before, to coordinate with the rich colour of the vase.

Prepare the fabric and mark the position of the vase as on page 35. Use the positioning diagrams on page 35, and stencil the background flowers in pale peach and the foreground flowers in mid pink and mid orange. Stencil leaf sprigs at random, sometimes using the full sprig and sometimes just four of the leaves. Stencil the vase in France Blue.

Stitching the cushion

Use 3340 orange or 3341 light orange for the mid orange flowers and 957 pink or 3326 light pink for the mid pink flowers. Refer to the stitch details below. Make up the piped cushion cover as before.

Stem stitch the leaf stems and veins in green.

Highlight just the base of the petals with stem stitch and satin stitch the centre.

Outline the petals with backstitch.

Work running stitch round the petals and emphasize the bases with straight stitches. Fill the centre with French knots.

IVY WREATH

THE RICH GREEN OF WINDING IVY STEMS AND GLEAMING RED BERRIES FORM FLOWING DESIGNS TO STITCH AND STENCIL ON TABLE LINENS.

IVY TABLECLOTH

A circular wreath of winding ivy and berries, stencilled onto a plain white cloth, forms a graceful table centrepiece.

This lovely circular ivy wreath can be stencilled and stitched onto a ready-made tablecloth. A circle is marked out in the centre of the cloth, then the large ivy sprig is repeated six times on the marked line to create a circular wreath.

The design is enhanced with back-stitch and stem stitch outlines on the stems and leaves, and the berries are worked in red satin stitch. The finished design measures 15¾in (40cm) in diameter, and is suitable for all but the smallest tablecloth.

Preparing the stencil

The diagram (right) shows the complete ivy stencil. For the tablecloth you will be using just the large sprig, shown here in colour. Before you start, mask off the berry cutouts.

Preparing the fabric

Fold the tablecloth in half in both directions to find the centre. Holding the end of the tape measure at the centre point, and pivoting it as you work, use the air-soluble pen to mark the fabric at intervals 6¾in (17cm) from the centre point, giving a circle 13½in (34cm) in diameter.

STENCILLING THE DESIGN

1 Position the stencil on the circle with the stems on the marked line. Stencil the leaves and stems with mid green paint. ▲

2 Reposition the stems on the circle close to the first sprig, and stencil again. Repeat around the circle, stencilling the sprig six times in all. Remove the masking tape and clean the stencil. ▲

3 Mask off the leaves. Realign the cutout over one stencilled sprig. Stencil the berries with Cardinal Red, then dry brush over the stems lightly with the same paint. Leave to dry, then set the paint with a hot iron. ◀

STITCHING THE TABLECLOTH

Mount the tablecloth in the embroidery hoop, and move the hoop around as you complete each section. Using a single strand each of light green and medium green cotton (floss) in the needle together, outline the leaves in backstitch and work the veins in straight stitch. Using two strands of brown, outline the stems in stem stitch – outline some stems all around, and outline others along one edge only. With two strands of red, satin stitch the berries.

Stem stitch round the stems using brown. On some stems, just stitch along one edge.

Fill the berries with satin stitch using red embroidery cotton (floss).

Backstitch around the leaves using one strand each of light green and medium green together in the needle.

Work the veins in straight stitch using one strand each of light green and medium green.

IVY NAPKINS

The small ivy sprig, stencilled and embroidered to coordinate with the tablecloth, fits neatly onto the corner of a napkin. Embellish ready-made napkins or make your own – simply stitch a double ⅜in (1cm) hem all around each fabric square. You will need the stencilling equipment listed on page 40, white fabric paint and the threads (floss) in the colour key below.

Mask off any cutouts close to the small ivy sprig. Position the cutout in one corner of the napkin and stencil the design in white.

COLOUR KEY	
COLOURS	SKEINS
☐ White	1
☐ 703 Light green	1
☐ 817 Red	1
☐ 905 Medium green	1

STITCHING THE SPRIG

Using two strands of white, satin stitch the stems. Outline the leaves in stem stitch and work straight stitches for the veins using two strands of light or medium green. Work French knots for the berries in red using all six strands of cotton (floss).

BRIGHT IDEAS

NAPKIN RING

This ivy napkin ring, made from green felt and brown cord, is the perfect finishing touch for your table linen set. Using an air-soluble fabric marker, draw around the inside of a large ivy leaf cutout onto green felt. Cut out four times. Sandwich one end of the brown cord between two felt leaves. With green sewing thread (floss), machine stitch the leaves together around the edges and across the centre for a veined effect. Repeat at the other end of the cord.
Tie around the napkin.

LAVENDER AND ROSES

PRETTILY EMBROIDERED CUSHIONS, FILLED WITH FRAGRANT LAVENDER AND ROSEBUDS, ENSURE PEACEFUL SLEEP AND A DELICATELY PERFUMED ROOM.

PERFUMED SLUMBER PILLOWS

Drift gently off to sleep with the soothing scent of lavender and roses, captured inside small embroidered pillows.

YOU WILL NEED

* ⅞yd (80cm) of 42in (112cm) wide fine white pure cotton fabric, washed and ironed
* Pearl fabric paints in Lapis-lazuli, Peridot and Tourmaline
* Stencil and stencil brush
* Large white saucer
* Kitchen paper and wallpaper lining paper
* Masking tape
* Dressmaker's chalk
* Tracing paper and pencil
* Dressmaker's carbon paper
* DMC stranded cottons/floss as listed in the colour key
* Pink and purple ribbon
* Embroidery needle, size 9
* Embroidery hoop
* White sewing thread
* Polyester stuffing
* Dried lavender and rosebuds

COLOUR KEY

COLOURS		SKEINS
For the lavender:		
	209 Mid lilac	1
	211 Pale lilac	1
	333 Dark lavender	1
	340 Pale lavender	1
	368 Green	1
	552 Dark lilac	1
For the rosebuds:		
	471 Dark green	1
	772 Pale green	1
	776 Rose pink	1
	963 Pale pink	1
	3348 Mid green	1

These small cushions are filled with fragrant dried rosebuds and lavender flowers to impart a delicate aroma and aid restful sleep. Made in crisp, pure white cotton, the covers are stencilled and embroidered with either a bunch of rosebuds or sprigs of lavender, and finished with a ribbon bow. The inner pads are filled with stuffing mixed with dried lavender or rosebuds. The finished cushions measure 10in (25cm) square.

Preparing the stencil

The diagram (below) shows the rosebud and lavender stencil. You will need all the cutouts, so mask off any cutouts close to the one you are using.

Preparing the fabric

Cut two 15in (38cm) squares of white cotton (floss). Use the dressmaker's chalk to draw a 10¾in (27cm) square in the centre of each. Trace off the lavender and rosebud stems (right) and transfer one onto each fabric square using the carbon paper. Centre the stems, with the base of the rosebud stems 3½in (9cm), and the lavender stems 2¾in (7cm) above the bottom line.

STENCILLING THE LAVENDER

1 Centre the group of three lavender flowers on the break in the first stem and stencil in Lapis-lazuli. Stencil the next set of flowers at the top of the stem. Repeat as required. Stencil each stem in this way. Clean and dry the stencil and brush. ➤

2 Position the two-flower lavender cutout over the first stencilled group of three flowers. Stencil in lapis-lazuli. Move the cutout and repeat to the top of the stem. Allow the paint to dry and set it with a hot iron. ◀

STENCILLING THE ROSEBUDS

1 Place the rosebud cutout at the top of a stem and stencil with tourmaline paint. Repeat to stencil a bud at the top of each stem. Allow the paint to dry.

2 Overlay the calyx cutout on the lower part of each bud and stencil in peridot. Stencil a single leaf on some stems. Allow the paint to dry and set it with a hot iron. ➤

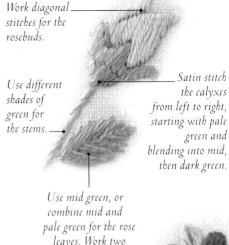

Work diagonal stitches for the rosebuds.

Use different shades of green for the stems.

Satin stitch the calyxes from left to right, starting with pale green and blending into mid, then dark green.

Use mid green, or combine mid and pale green for the rose leaves. Work two bands to create the vein.

For the groups of two flowers use a paler colour than the groups of three.

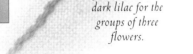

Use dark lavender, pale lavender or dark lilac for the groups of three flowers.

STITCHING THE FLOWERS

Refer to the stitch details (above). Stitch the lavender flowers with satin and lazy daisy stitch, using two colours on each stem. Work the stems in stem stitch. Work the lazy daisy stitches with three strands of cotton (floss), and the rest of the embroidery with two strands.

Use two strands of cotton (floss) for the rosebuds. Satin stitch the buds in pale pink or rose pink and sometimes a strand of each. Satin stitch the calyxes and leaves using three shades of green.

Making the covers

Trim the fabric to the marked lines. See page 61 for making up the cushion covers, taking ⅜in (1cm) seams.

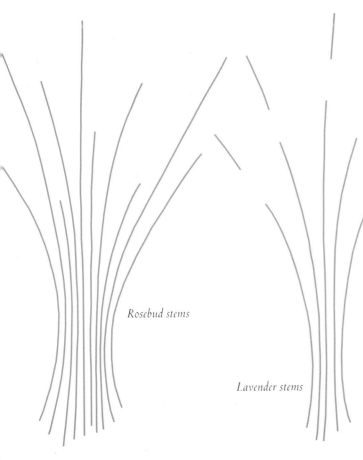

Rosebud stems

Lavender stems

FLANGED CUSHION

A delicate scattering of rosebuds and lavender sprigs decorate this pretty cushion cover, made to fit a 12in (30cm) square cushion pad.

The design is perfect for bedroom scatter cushions. You could also use the stencils on a plain duvet cover to complete a delightful bedroom set.

YOU WILL NEED

❋ ¾yd (60cm) of 42in (112cm) wide fine white pure cotton fabric, washed and ironed

❋ Fabric paints, DMC stranded cottons/floss, and stencilling and sewing equipment as listed on page 44

❋ Cushion pad, 12in (30cm) square

BRIGHT IDEAS

ORGANZA SACHETS

Create exquisite fragrant sachets using white organza. Draw a 12 x 11in (30 x 28cm) rectangle on paper and tape the organza on top. Stencil rosebuds or lavender sprigs within the rectangle and embroider them with the cottons (floss) listed in the colour key on page 44. Cut out the organza to the size of the rectangle. Right sides together, stitch the shorter sides, centre the seam at the back and stitch across the bottom, then turn through to the right side. Fold a narrow double hem at the top and secure it with running stitch. Fill with rosebuds or dried lavender and tie with a ribbon.

STENCILLING THE CUSHION

Cut a 19in (48cm) square of white fabric and mark a 17¼in (44cm) square in the centre. Using the paint colours listed on page 44 and working within the marked square, randomly stencil the rosebuds and lavender sprigs as shown on page 45, scattering them in different directions. Allow the paint to dry and set it with a hot iron.

FINISHING THE CUSHION

Embroider the flowers following the stitching instructions on page 45. Trim the fabric to the marked line, then refer to page 61 to make up the cover, taking ⅜in (1cm) seam allowances. To create the flanged border, machine stitch through both layers 2¼in (6cm) in from the outer edge of the cover.

CUTWORK ROSES

THE SLENDER BEAUTIES OF ART NOUVEAU
ROSES, STENCILLED ON BRIGHT FABRICS,
MAKE ELEGANT SUBJECTS FOR THE
DELICATE ART OF CUTWORK.

ROSE CURTAINS

Gauzy panels with slender stencilled roses and cutwork embroidery make a beautiful window treatment.

YOU WILL NEED

* Fine cotton voile or muslin in pink and orange
* Fabric paint in Tourmaline Pearl
* Stencil and stencil brush
* Fine square-ended water colour brush
* Large white saucer
* Kitchen paper and wallpaper lining paper
* Spray mount
* DMC stranded cotton/floss as listed in the colour key
* Embroidery needle, size 9
* Embroidery hoop
* Sharp pointed embroidery scissors
* Sewing threads to match the fabric

COLOUR KEY

COLOUR	SKEINS
894 Salmon pink	1

Floaty pink fabric panels, stencilled and delicately stitched, alternate with slimmer panels of plain orange fabric in this beautiful window treatment. As light floods through the window, the cutwork takes on a deceptively fragile appearance – in fact, the fabric paint, concealed by the stitching, prevents fraying and supports the embroidery.

The panels are finished with hand-stitched hems and can be threaded onto a curtain rod. If you prefer, make them up in different colours to suit your room; simply use fabric paint and stranded cottons (floss) to match your chosen fabric colour.

The finished cutwork panels are 11in (27.5cm) wide and the plain ones 8in (20cm) wide.

Preparing the stencil

The diagram (right) shows the complete Art Nouveau rose stencil. The stencil is quite fragile, so handle it with care. You will be using all the cutouts for the curtains, so mask off any nearby cutouts before you start. Spray mount the back of the stencil and leave it to dry.

Preparing the panels

Measure the width and height of the window. For the cut fabric length, add on 2in (5cm) for a hem at the bottom, and enough for a casing at the top to thread the panels onto a curtain rod. Cut the appropriate number of 12in (30cm) wide pink panels and 9in (22.5cm) wide orange panels. Fold each pink panel in half lengthwise; crease a centre line on the lower 18in (46cm).

STENCILLING THE CURTAIN

1 Tape a pink panel to the prepared work surface with masking tape. Centre the rose cutout on the crease with the base of the stem 6in (15cm) above the bottom edge of the fabric. Stencil with tourmaline pearl fabric paint. Stencil all the pink panels in this way. ▶

2 Gently lift the stencil off the fabric. Using the fine square-ended brush, fill in the bridges with tourmaline pearl fabric paint. Allow to dry, then set the paint with a hot iron. ◀

STITCHING THE CUTWORK

It is essential to use a hoop to prevent the fine fabric puckering. Use a single strand of 894 salmon pink cotton (floss) throughout and refer to the stitch details (right) and to pages 51–52.

Finishing the curtain

Fold and hand stitch ¼in (6mm) double hems down the sides of all the panels. Along the bottom edges, fold and hand stitch a 1in (2.5cm) double hem, 4in (10cm) from the bottom of the design. Stitch a channel at the top of each panel. Thread the cutwork and plain panels alternately onto the curtain rod and hang them.

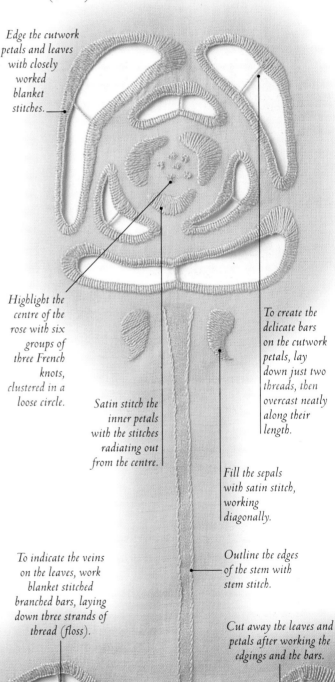

Edge the cutwork petals and leaves with closely worked blanket stitches.

Highlight the centre of the rose with six groups of three French knots, clustered in a loose circle.

To create the delicate bars on the cutwork petals, lay down just two threads, then overcast neatly along their length.

Satin stitch the inner petals with the stitches radiating out from the centre.

Fill the sepals with satin stitch, working diagonally.

To indicate the veins on the leaves, work blanket stitched branched bars, laying down three strands of thread (floss).

Outline the edges of the stem with stem stitch.

Cut away the leaves and petals after working the edgings and the bars.

ROSE MAT

The inner part of the rose and a leaf are repeated in a circular cutwork design on this bright mat. The design, worked on orange fabric, is beautifully set off by the bright pink backing. The finished mat has a bound edge to match the backing, and is 12½in (32cm) in diameter.

YOU WILL NEED

❋ Orange cotton fabric, 16in (40cm) square

❋ ⅜yd (30cm) pink cotton fabric

❋ Fabric paint in Transparent Bright Orange

❋ DMC stranded cotton/floss as listed in the colour key

❋ Stencilling and embroidery equipment as listed on page 48

❋ Air-soluble fabric marker and masking tape

❋ Tape measure

COLOUR KEY

COLOUR	SKEINS
741 Orange	1

STENCILLING THE DESIGN

1 Position the central vein of one leaf on a crease, 1½in (4cm) from the centre. Stencil it in transparent bright orange paint. Repeat on alternate creases.

2 On the remaining creases, place the rose 1½in (4cm) from the centre and stencil it in transparent bright orange. Fill in the bridges as in step 2, page 49. When the paint is dry, set it with a hot iron.

Preparing the stencil

The diagram (right) shows the complete Art Nouveau rose stencil. For the mat you will be using the leaves and the inner petals, shown here in colour. You will be using the leaf first, so mask off all the other cutouts before you start.

STITCHING THE MAT

Work the cutwork as shown on page 49 but use one strand of 741 orange. Then cut out the fabric along the marked circle. Cut a circle of pink fabric the same size and place them wrong sides together. Cut and join enough pink 1in (2.5cm) wide bias strips to make 1¼yd (1m) of ½in (12mm) wide bias binding. Use it to bind the edge of the mat.

On the branched bars, take care to align the blanket stitch ridges.

Preparing the fabric

Fold the orange fabric square in half both ways to find the centre. With the end of a tape measure at the centre, use the air-soluble fabric marker to draw a circle with a 6¼in (16cm) radius. Press out the foldlines. Fold the fabric in half and then into three to give six creases. Unfold the fabric.

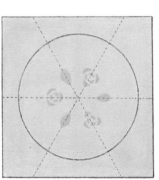

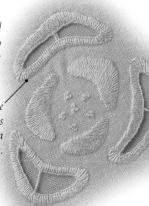

Position the blanket stitches accurately for a smooth line.

ROSE CUTWORK TECHNIQUE

With its delicate lacy finish, cutwork is one of the prettiest forms of embroidery. The open effect is achieved by edging the design with blanket stitch and cutting away the background. The technique of cutwork embroidery is perfect for floral and foliage designs and is traditionally used to embellish clothing, tablewear and bedding.

The design is marked on the fabric with parallel lines and then outlined in running stitch. For a sharp outline and to prevent fraying, the blanket stitches are worked very closely together, with the ridges towards the areas to be cut away.

When large areas of fabric are to be cut away, the open spaces are made prettier and stronger by working bars across them (see overleaf). Always work the bars first, then add the edgings afterwards.

Practise on a firm fabric which does not fray easily, such as cotton or closely woven linen, before progressing to the fine cotton and muslin used for the cutwork roses on the previous pages. For the embroidery, use a fine embroidery needle and one or two strands of stranded cotton (embroidery floss). Before starting to stitch, mount the fabric in a hoop.

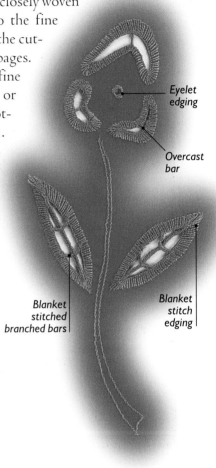

Eyelet edging

Overcast bar

Blanket stitched branched bars

Blanket stitch edging

EYELET EDGING

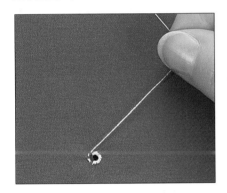

Outline a circle with a single row of running stitch. Pierce the centre of the circle with a knitting needle or stiletto, making the hole slightly smaller than the circle. Overcast over the running stitches, pulling the thread tight with each stitch and keeping your thumb firmly over the circle so that it doesn't get pulled out of shape.

BLANKET STITCH EDGING

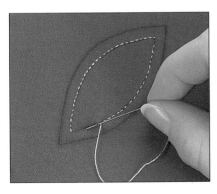

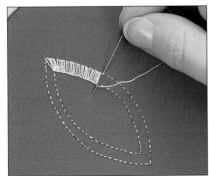

1 Transfer the design on to the fabric. If desired, mark the areas to be cut away. Mount the fabric in a hoop and work running stitch along the inner and the outer marked lines of the design.

2 Work blanket stitch over the two stitched lines, as on page 80, with the ridged edge of the stitch towards the edge to be cut. Cut away the fabric in the centre, as shown overleaf.

WHAT WENT WRONG

Bendy bars
Working bars too tightly pulls them out of shape and causes them to hover above the fabric. For perfectly formed bars that lie flat on the fabric, always use an embroidery hoop and keep the tension of the stitches even.

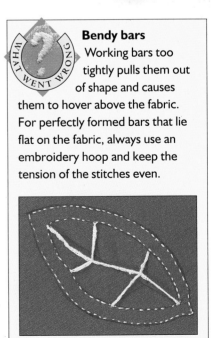

OVERCAST BARS

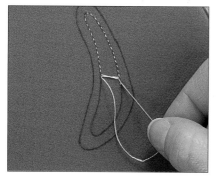

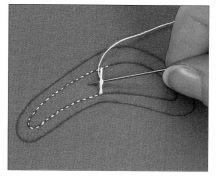

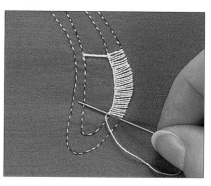

1 Work running stitch along the inner marked line. At the desired position for the bar, take the thread across to the opposite marked line and secure it with a tiny stitch. Lay down two more threads in the same way.

2 Overcast along the length of the bar by wrapping the thread around it. Pull the thread tight with each stitch and be careful not to pierce the fabric.

3 Finish outlining the inner and the outer marked line with running stitch. Work a blanket stitch edging, as shown on the previous page, then cut away the fabric, as shown (below).

BLANKET STITCHED BRANCHED BARS

CUTTING AWAY

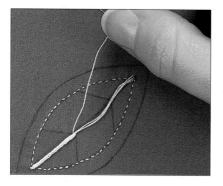

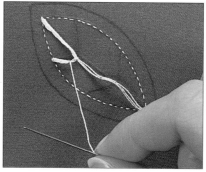

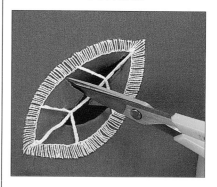

1 Follow step 1 (above) to make a central bar. Then work closely worked blanket stitch from left to right across one third of the bar, keeping the ridged edge of the stitches beneath the bar, as shown.

2 Lay down three threads, from the central bar to the bottom left of the inner marked line; work the securing stitch at the centre into the central bar. Then work blanket stitch across the threads from left to right.

1 Carefully working underneath a bar or in the centre of an edged motif, make the initial cuts from the right side, snipping across the centre and then outwards to the edges.

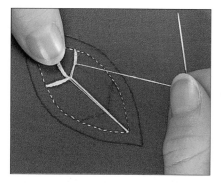

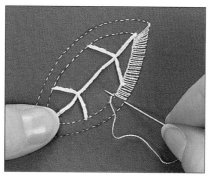

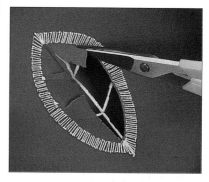

3 Lay down three strands from the central bar to the top left of the inner marked line. Then work blanket stitch across them from right to left.

4 Continue working blanket stitch along the central bar, making branched bars as required. Complete the running stitch outlines and work a blanket stitch edging, as shown on the previous page. Cut away the fabric, as shown (right).

2 Turn the work to the wrong side and cut the fabric close to the stitching. Stroke any stubborn threads away from the edge and trim them neatly.

BAMBOO TRELLIS

A TRELLIS OF KNOTTED BAMBOO FRAMES
DELICATELY EMBROIDERED, BLUSH PINK
APPLE BLOSSOMS TO CELEBRATE
THE JOYS OF SPRING.

BAMBOO TRELLIS BLIND

An interlocking trellis of bamboo makes a perfect frame for scattered apple blossoms.

COLOUR KEY

COLOURS	SKEINS
White	1
744 Yellow	1
776 Deep pink	1
783 Gold	1
818 Light pink	1
987 Dark green	1

PAINT COLOUR GUIDE

For the bamboo: use Raw Sienna.

For the apple blossom: mix White with a tiny touch of Transparent Bengal Pink to make very pale pink. Make a slightly darker pink by adding a little more Transparent Bengal Pink to White.

For the leaves: use Light Green.

The bamboo and blossom stencil is used to create a large repeating border design for a simple roller blind. You'll need to draw up a grid on cardboard first (see below right) to use as a guide for the trellis.

The blind is stencilled and then lightly embroidered with simple stitches before it is made up using a roller blind kit; read through the measuring up instructions in the pack before you buy the fabric.

The blind shown here is made from a single fabric width and measures 43in (109cm) wide. For a wider blind, choose wider fabric and extend the width of the trellis.

Preparing the stencil

The diagram (right) shows the complete stencil. The blind uses all the cutouts — the leaves, bamboo and blossom. Spray mount the back of the stencil and leave it to dry.

Drawing up the grid

With the pencil, ruler and set square, draw a grid of six 7in (18cm) squares in two rows of three. Using the black marker pen draw both diagonals through each square. The grid fits twice across the fabric width.

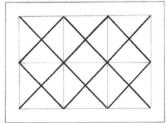

STENCILLING THE BAMBOO TRELLIS

1 Crease the fabric 4¾in (12cm) from the cut edge – this edge will be the bottom of the blind. Unfold it and tape it to the prepared work surface with the selvedges vertical and the creased edge at the bottom.

2 Place the drawn grid under the fabric, 3¼in (8cm) in from the left edge and the lower points of the grid resting on the crease. Using the grid as a positioning guide, dry brush the first bamboo length in raw sienna.

3 Reposition the cutout to cross the first stencilled bamboo length and stencil as before. Continue in this way until the trellis is complete. ▼

4 Move the drawn grid to the right, making sure the lower points rest on the crease and the left-hand edge of the grid matches the right-hand edge of the stencilled trellis. Repeat steps **2** and **3** to stencil the second half of the trellis.

5 Use very pale pink to stencil a single flower in alternate spaces of the trellis. Use the darker pink to stencil a second flower in each section, overlapping the first. Repeat to create clusters of overlapping flowers. Wash and dry the brush and stencil. ▼

6 Stencil the leaves in light green, fitting them to the curves of the flower petals. Allow to dry, then set all the paints with a hot iron. ▼

Outline the flowers in stem stitch, using white or light pink for the lighter ones and deep pink for the darker ones.

Indicate the flower stamens with long yellow straight stitches radiating out from the centre.

Work a single gold French knot at the tip of each stamen.

A cluster of gold French knots indicates the centre of some of the flowers.

Fill some leaves with open fishbone stitch.

EMBROIDERING THE BLOSSOM

Mount the fabric in the embroidery hoop, use two strands of cotton (floss) throughout, and refer to the stitch details (right). Outline some of the flowers in stem stitch using white, 776 deep pink and 818 light pink. Represent the stamens with straight stitches radiating out from the centres in 744 yellow. Using 783 gold, work a single French knot at the end of each stamen and work a cluster in the centre of some of the flowers. Fill some of the leaves with open fishbone stitch using 987 dark green cotton (floss).

Making up the blind

Follow the instructions in the roller blind kit to make up the blind. When you are hemming the sides and base, make sure that the trellis comes right to the folded edges.

TRELLIS CUSHION

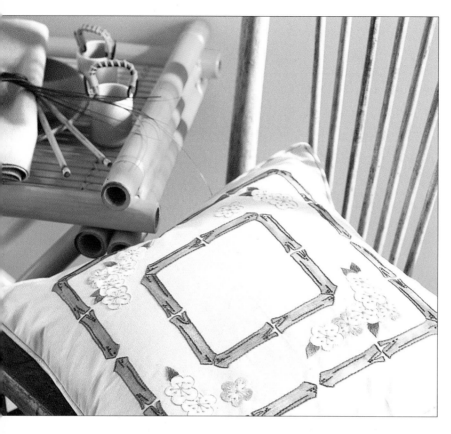

The bamboo creates a frame to display clusters of blossoms on this unusual cushion cover. The cover fits a 15in (38cm) square cushion pad. You will need ⅝yd (50cm) of fabric, 1⅞yd (1.70m) of piping, and the paints, stencilling equipment and stranded cottons (floss) listed on page 54, plus one skein each of 989 mid green, 433 mid brown and 898 dark brown.

Preparing the fabric

Cut a 16½in (42cm) square of fabric and crease it lightly along both diagonals. Unfold, then fold it in half both ways and crease lightly. Open the fabric out and tape it to the work surface.

Work the stamens in yellow straight stitches, and add gold French knots at the tips.

STENCILLING THE DESIGN

1 For the outer frame, place the bamboo cutout with each end touching a diagonal crease. Dry brush it with raw sienna paint. Repeat three times to make a square. ▶

On some of the darker flowers, use long and short stitch to blend deep pink into light pink.

Stem stitch the outlines of some flowers. Use light pink or deep pink, depending on the flower colour.

Use mid brown and stem stitch to outline the bamboo.

Use dark brown for the stem stitched ridges and the French knots.

Fill some of the lighter flowers with long and short stitch, blending light pink into white.

2 Mask off half of the bamboo cutout and repeat step 1 to create a smaller inner square. Add clusters of blossoms and leaves, following steps 5-6 on the previous page. Allow to dry, then set all the paints with a hot iron. ▶

Fill the leaves with long and short stitch, blending mid and dark green.

EMBROIDERING THE CUSHION COVER

Use two strands of cotton (floss) and refer to the stitch details. Fill some flowers with long and short stitch. Outline the others in stem stitch. Straight stitch the stamens and add French knots. Fill the leaves with long and short stitch, blending the two shades of green. Stem stitch the bamboo outlines and add French knots.

Making up the cover

See page 61 and page 36 for the piping.

GYPSOPHILA

SPRAYS OF TINY FLOWERS AND LEAVES ON DAINTILY
BRANCHED STALKS ARE STENCILLED IN WHITE ON
NATURAL LINEN AND DELICATELY ENHANCED
WITH SIMPLE EMBROIDERY.

YOU WILL NEED

- ❈ 1⅝yd (150cm) of 59in (150cm) wide beige linen
- ❈ Fabric paint in White
- ❈ Stencil and stencil brush
- ❈ Kitchen paper and wallpaper lining paper
- ❈ Tape measure
- ❈ Masking tape
- ❈ Dark tacking thread and needle
- ❈ Tracing paper and pencil
- ❈ Air-soluble fabric marker
- ❈ White or yellow dressmaker's carbon paper
- ❈ DMC stranded cotton/floss as listed in the colour key
- ❈ Embroidery needle, size 8
- ❈ Embroidery hoop
- ❈ Sewing thread to match the linen
- ❈ Sewing needle

COLOUR KEY

COLOUR	SKEINS
☐ B5200 Brilliant white	2

GYPSOPHILA LINEN

Dainty sprigs of gypsophila flow along the edge of a circular tablecloth and cluster in a central wreath.

The circular cloth is the perfect cover for a side table in an elegant, understated bedroom. The cloth is folded into equal segments and the creases are used to position the stalks – these are given as a tracing (right). The blooms are stencilled in white and each sprig is delicately embroidered in a variety of simple stitches.

The finished tablecloth measures 38½in (100cm) in diameter. The fabric quantity quoted here includes enough extra linen to make the piped cushion cover (see overleaf).

Preparing the stencil

The diagram (below) shows the complete gypsophila stencil. For the tablecloth, you need just the smaller cluster of blooms and leaves, shown here in grey. Before stencilling, mask off any cutouts close by.

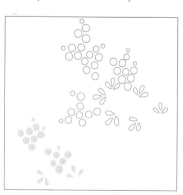

Trace off the stalks (left) and transfer them on to the linen before starting to stencil, as explained in step 1 (right).

Preparing the fabric

Cut a 43in (110cm) square of the beige linen. Fold it in half both ways, then fold it in half diagonally and press the folds. Unfold the linen, which should now have eight creases meeting at the centre. Use the air-soluble fabric marker to make a series of dots, 20in (52cm) from the centre. Join the marks with a tacked circle. Then make a series of dots 3¼in (8cm) from the centre and join them with another tacked circle.

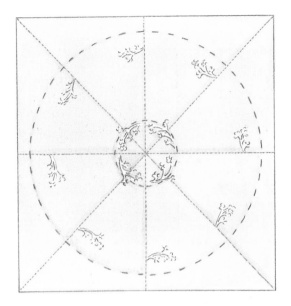

STENCILLING THE SPRIGS

1 Trace the stalks (left). Place the tracing so the stalk curves outwards, with the end on a crease, 5¼in (13cm) from the outer circle. Tilt it so the tip is 3¼in (8cm) from the outer circle. Transfer it with the dressmaker's carbon paper. Repeat seven times to transfer the stalks at each crease. ▼

Work the stems first using three strands of cotton (floss) and stem stitch.

2 For the central wreath, position the curve of the stalk tracing on the inner circle with the end against a crease, and the stalk curving inwards. Transfer the stalks as before. Repeat three more times, spacing the stalks evenly. ▲

3 To stencil the outer border, make sure the cutout is facing the right way, and position it over one traced stalk. Stencil the flowers and leaves with white paint. Repeat at each traced stalk. ▼

4 For the central wreath, rotate the cutout so that the flowers face inwards. Position it over each stalk and stencil in white. Allow the paint to dry and set it with a hot iron.

EMBROIDERING

Use three strands of cotton (floss) for the stalks and two for the flowers and leaves. Refer to the stitch details (left). Stem stitch the stalks and satin stitch the leaves. Straight or blanket stitch some flowers with the stitches radiating out from the centre.

Finishing off

Trim the fabric along the outer tacked line. Remove all the tacking, then handstitch a ⅜in (1cm) double hem.

Stitch some flowers with radiating straight stitches, using two strands of cotton (floss).

Leave some flowers as a paint effect to provide a variety of texture.

On other flowers, work blanket stitches radiating out from the centre. Extend the stitches beyond the paint.

GYPSOPHILA CUSHION

The large gypsophila spray can be repeated to create a cloud of tiny blooms and leaves. Interpreted once more in white, it makes a lovely design for a cushion to complement the tablecloth. The cushion cover fits a pad 15¾in (40cm) square. You will need the fabric left over from the table-cloth, 1.70m (1⅞yd) of piping, and the stencilling and embroidery equipment listed on page 58.

Preparing the stencil

For the cushion, you will be using only the larger flower spray cutout, shown in grey on the diagram (below). Before you start stencilling, mask off any nearby cutouts.

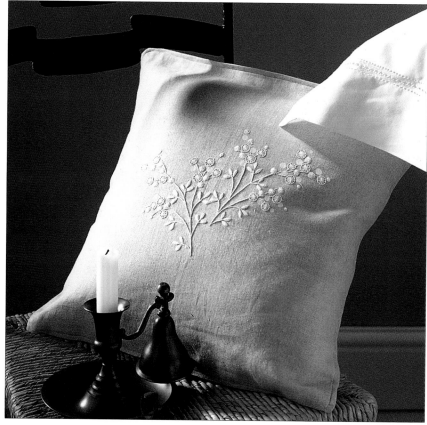

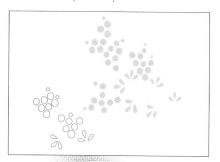

Leave some flowers unstitched.

Work the stems with three strands of cotton (floss) and stem stitch.

Using two strands, cover some of the flowers with radiating blanket stitches or straight stitches.

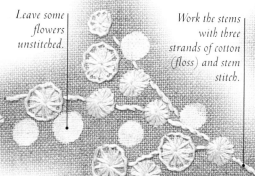

STITCHING

Embroider the design as for the tablecloth on page 59. Trim the embroidered panel to 17in (43cm) square. Make up the cushion cover referring to page 61, and page 36 for the piping.

STENCILLING

1 Cut a 17¾in (45cm) square of beige linen. Fold it in half, crease it lightly, then unfold it. Trace the stalks from the picture (left).

2 Angle the tracing to the left, and place the end on the fold, 6¼in (16cm) from the bottom of the fabric. Transfer it with carbon paper. Flip it and transfer it again, just above the first stalks as shown. ▼

3 Place the large spray cutout over the bottom stalk; stencil it in white. Clean, dry and flip the stencil, then stencil the second stalk. Leave to dry and set the paint with a hot iron.

EASY CUSHION COVERS

The easiest type of cushion cover to make is a square or rectangular shape with an overlapped back opening. Use fabrics that are closely woven, crease-resistant and durable. Strong furnishing fabrics made of cotton and linen blends are ideal. See the 'You Will Need' boxes for fabric recommendations for each of the projects involving cushions.

Cut out the front and back pieces of the cover separately, and stencil and work the design before assembling the cushion. You could stitch a small piece of needlepoint on to the cover before assembling instead; larger pieces can form the whole cushion front, in which case you'll need fabric for the back piece only.

To hold the pad firmly in place, the cushion cover needs a generous overlap at the back. The steps below explain how to make a cover with a 4in (10cm) wide overlap, which suits cushions up to 13¾in (35cm) square. For larger cushions, the overlap needs to be at least 6in (15cm), so cut the back piece 8¼in (21cm) wider than the front.

To ensure that the cushion holds its shape when in use, always position the back overlap on a rectangular cover so that it runs widthwise (parallel to the two shorter sides).

When you have finished stitching the cover (step **4** below), turn it to the right side and insert the pad.

MAKING A CUSHION WITH AN OVERLAPPED OPENING

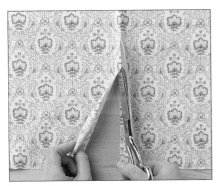

1 Cut the fabric for the front piece ⅝in (1.5cm) larger all round than the finished cushion. Cut the fabric for the back piece 6¼in (16cm) wider than the front. Cut the back piece in half widthwise.

2 Turn, press and machine stitch a ⅝in (1.5cm) double hem along the centre edge of each back piece.

3 With right sides together, pin the back pieces to the front. Make sure that the raw edges match all round and the hemmed centre back edges overlap by about 4in (10cm).

4 Stitch around the outer edge, taking ⅝in (1.5cm) seam allowances. Stitch twice across each end of the overlap for strength. Trim the corners of seam allowances diagonally.

STITCH LIBRARY

THIS CHAPTER CONTAINS ALL THE STITCHES USED IN THE PROJECTS, GROUPED TOGETHER FOR EASE OF REFERENCE.

SATIN STITCH

Starting and finishing off satin stitch

When you have finished satin stitching a motif, always secure the thread ends and trim them off before working the next motif. Don't trail the thread across the back of the work to start another motif – it may show through as a shadow on your finished work, especially on lightweight or pale fabric.

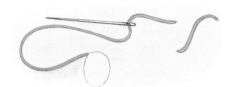

1 A little way from your starting point, push the needle through to the back of the fabric, leaving a 3in (7.5cm) tail of thread on the right side. Bring the needle out to the front again at your starting point on the edge of the motif.

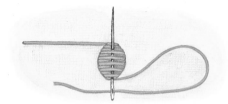

2 When you have filled in the motif, take the thread through to the back. Weave it into the back of your stitching, and trim it off close to the surface. Then pull the first thread end to the wrong side, weave it in and trim it off in the same way.

Filling a rounded shape with basic satin stitch

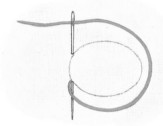

1 Bring the needle out at the front of the fabric at the edge of the shape. Insert the needle at the opposite edge, and bring it out again next to where you started.

2 Pull the thread through gently, so that it runs straight between the marked lines without wavering; it should lie smoothly against the surface of the fabric, without puckering it.

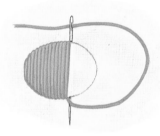

3 Repeat steps 1-2, keeping the stitches parallel and close together so that they lie neatly and evenly on the surface of the fabric.

Working a basic satin stitch line

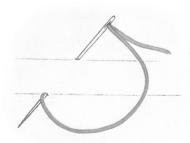

1 Bring the needle out at the front of the fabric at the lower marked line. Take the thread upwards and insert the needle on the top row, at a 45° angle to the marked line; bring it out again next to where you started.

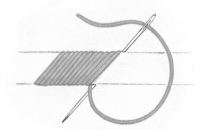

2 Work parallel, closely spaced stitches along the row, keeping them at exactly the same angle and placing the needle precisely on the marked lines to create even edges.

WHAT WENT WRONG?

Loose stitches
Loose, untidy satin stitches are created when working the stitch over an area which is too large. For the best results, each stitch should be no more than ⅜-½in (10-12mm) long. For large areas use encroaching satin stitch, worked in manageable rows.

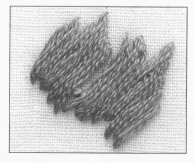

Working surface satin stitch

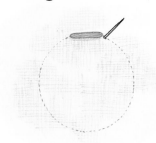 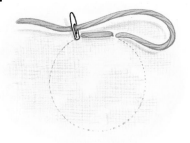 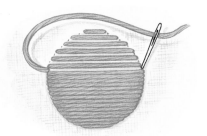

1 Bring the thread to the front and work a stitch straight across the shape with a stabbing motion. Bring the needle out again as close as possible to the end of the first stitch.

2 Insert the needle into the fabric straight across the shape in the opposite direction to form the next satin stitch. Repeat these two steps to fill the shape.

Alternatively, space the stitches slightly further apart and fill in with a second sequence of stitches.

STRAIGHT STITCH

Securing your starting thread

Finishing off

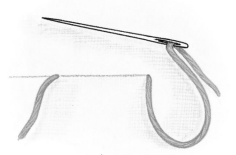 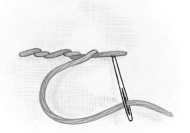 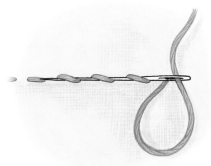

1 Push the needle to the back of the fabric, a little way from your starting point. Leave a short tail of thread at the front. Bring the needle to the front at your starting point.

2 As you work along the line, stitch over the thread at the back to secure it. Then pull the loose thread end through to the back and snip it off close to the surface.

To secure the thread end when you have finished, push the needle to the back of the fabric. Weave the thread into the back of several stitches and trim it off close to the surface.

Working basic straight stitch

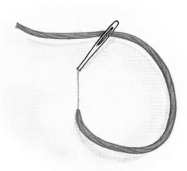  

To work an individual straight stitch, bring the needle out to the front. Push it through to the wrong side to make a single stitch of the required length.

To work a cluster of straight stitches, work individual straight stitches of varying lengths and in different directions according to the design.

To create a simple straight stitch flower, make as many straight stitches as desired, working outwards from a central circle or oval.

Working running stitch

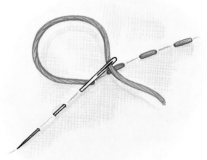

Working from right to left, bring the needle out to the front at your starting point. Pass the needle in and out of the fabric along the stitching line. Work several stitches at a time, keeping the length and tension even.

Double running stitch

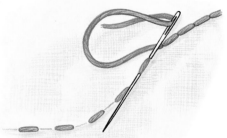

Work a row of evenly spaced running stitches along the stitching line, including any offshoot stitches. Turn the work round. Work another set of running stitches, filling in the spaces left by the first and using the same holes.

Straight stitch

Stem stitch

Backstitch

Running stitch

Working stem stitch

1 Work upwards, keeping the working thread to the right of the needle. Bring the needle out to the front and insert it a little way from your starting point. Bring it out again, half a stitch length back.

2 Insert the needle half a stitch length from the end of the previous stitch. Bring it out at the end of the previous stitch, through the same hole in the fabric. Continue in this way.

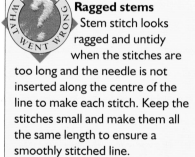

For a heavy stem stitch line, angle the needle slightly as you insert it, and work smaller stitches.

Working backstitch

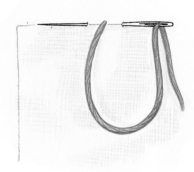

1 Working from right to left, bring the needle out to the front one stitch length from your starting point. Insert the needle at your starting point and bring it out again, two stitch lengths away.

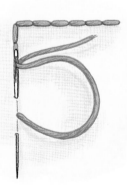

2 Pull the thread through to leave a single stitch at the front. Then repeat step 1, inserting the needle in the hole at the end of the previous stitch. Continue in this way, keeping all the stitches the same length.

Ragged stems
Stem stitch looks ragged and untidy when the stitches are too long and the needle is not inserted along the centre of the line to make each stitch. Keep the stitches small and make them all the same length to ensure a smoothly stitched line.

CROSS STITCH

Starting and finishing off

For a professional finish, always weave the loose ends of the yarn into the the back of the work. Don't tie a knot in the yarn – the knot will make a lump on the right side and may eventually work loose, so your stitching unravels.

1 Close to your starting point, push the needle through to the back of the fabric, leaving a 5cm (2in) thread end at the front. You will secure this later, when you have finished stitching the length of yarn.

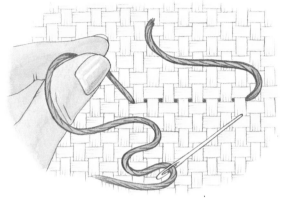

Joining in a new length

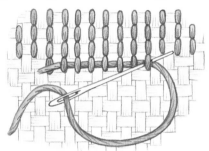

On the back of the fabric, run the new length of yarn under the back of several stitches close to where you are working. Then take a small backstitch over the last stitch and bring the needle out in the correct place at the front of the fabric.

2 When you have about 5cm (2in) of yarn left, or you've finished the colour block, take the needle through to the back and darn the yarn end under several stitches. Then pull the loose thread end at the start of your stitching through to the back and darn it in.

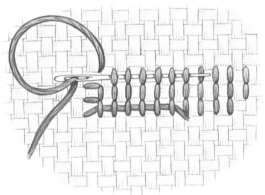

Working individual counted cross stitch

Bring the needle out at the front of the fabric and insert it one hole down and one hole to the right. Pull the thread through. Bring the needle out one hole to the left and insert it one hole up and one to the right.

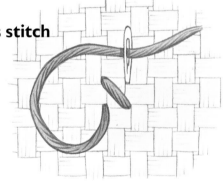

LAZY DAISY STITCH

Working lazy daisy stitch

1 Bring the needle through to the front of the fabric. Insert the needle beside the emerging thread and bring it out to the front again a stitch length away, looping the working thread under the point of the needle.

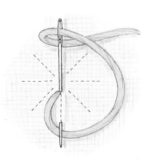

2 Pull the thread so that the loop lies flat. Make a short straight stitch over the loop to anchor it. Bring the needle out to the front ready to begin the next stitch.

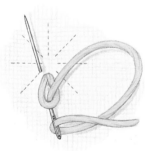

BLANKET STITCH

Securing the thread

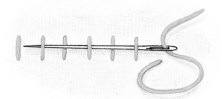

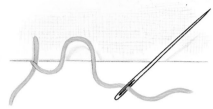

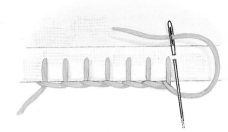

Method A Push the needle through to the front at your starting point, leaving a short tail of thread at the back. Work a few stitches, then turn the fabric over and weave the loose thread into the back of the stitches. To finish, fasten off the thread in the same way.

1 Method B Use this method for edging appliqué and fabric edges. To start, insert the needle at the top edge of the stitching line, leaving a tail of thread at the front. Take the working thread over the loose thread, ready to work the next stitch.

2 Work the row of stitches, then take the thread to the back. Make two or three tiny stitches on top of each other, next to the last upright and taking the needle through the background fabric only. Finish off the thread at the start in the same way.

Working blanket stitch for surface embroidery

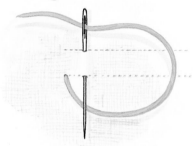

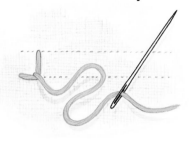

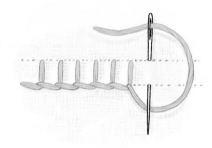

1 Bring the needle to the front on the lower line and insert it at the top, a little way to the right. Bring it out directly below, keeping the thread under the tip of the needle .

2 Pull the thread through the fabric, over the top of the working thread. Gently pull the thread to form a firm loop at the lower line.

3 Continue working in this way, spacing the upright stitches evenly and making them all the same height.

Working blanket stitch round a curved shape

1 Work blanket stitches round the shape, with the loops on the outside and the uprights facing towards the centre.

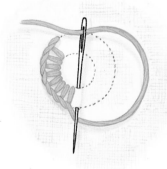

2 When you have stitched all round, work the last upright. Take the needle back through the fabric at the point where it originally emerged.

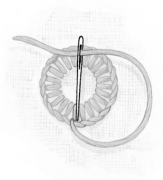

Messy stitches Untidy blanket stitch is the result of working unevenly spaced and sized stitches. Try to keep the stitches of an even length and space them out at equal intervals along the row.

FRENCH KNOT

Starting and finishing knotted stitches

When you are working individual knots or widely spaced knots, fasten off the thread after each knot. When working groups of closely spaced knots, you can carry the thread across the back of the fabric between knots, instead of fastening it off after every stitch.

To start, work two or three tiny stitches at the back of the fabric, positioning them where they will be covered by the embroidery stitch. To finish, fasten off the thread in the same way, directly beneath the knot. Trim the thread close to the fabric.

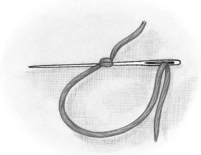

Working a French knot

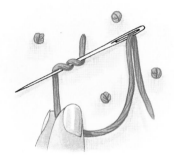 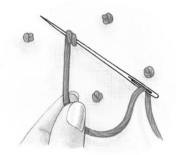 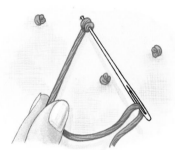

1 Bring the thread through to the front of the fabric. Holding the thread taut with your left hand, wrap it twice round the needle.

2 Pull the thread gently to tighten the twists round the needle. Don't overtighten the twists, or you will find it difficult to slide the needle through in the next step.

3 Still holding the thread taut with your left hand, insert the needle into the fabric close to the point where it originally emerged. Pull the needle and thread through to the back, to leave a loose knot at the front.

OPEN FISHBONE STITCH

Working open fishbone stitch

1 Mark two lines within the shape to keep the stitches even. Bring the needle to the front at 1 and take a slanting stitch to the right-hand edge at 2. Bring the needle out at 3 and take it to the back at 4. Bring it to the front at 5.

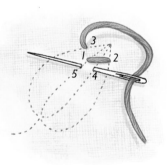

2 Continue working slanted stitches alternately from side to side until the shape is filled.

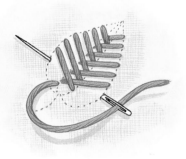

Poor shading
Colours that contrast too strongly produce visible dividing lines between each change of thread. For a subtle shaded effect, choose colours that are close in tone, and work each new colour into the spaces left by the previous row so that they blend well.

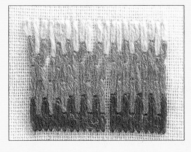

LONG AND SHORT STITCH

Working long and short stitch

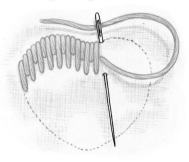 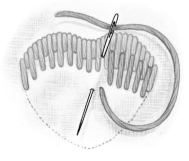

Long and short stitch in graduated shades suggests the delicate colouring of sweet peas.

1 Work the foundation row in alternate long and short stitches, working from left to right and following the outline of the shape to be filled. Work the stitches close together.

2 Work the second row from right to left, filling in the spaces left by the first row and keeping the stitches all the same length.

3 Work subsequent rows alternately from left to right and right to left, keeping all the stitches the same length, as in step **2**. Change thread colour as you work for a subtle blended effect and work stitches closely so no background fabric shows.

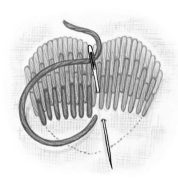

Changing the direction of long and short stitch

The direction in which long and short stitch is worked is very important in creating the right shaded effect within a design.

When working a flower design, fill each petal with stitches worked from base to tip for a natural-looking blend of colours. The first row of stitches can be fanned out for a radiating effect within each petal.

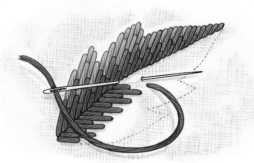

To create natural shading on a leaf, slant the stitches in opposite directions on each side of the central vein and use two or three shades of green.

STENCIL LIBRARY

All the materials you need to make the stencils are available from art and craft stores. It's best to use acetate because it lasts longer, you can see through it and it is easy to clean. Either trace the patterns, which are given actual size, directly from the book on to the acetate using a pencil, or use a photocopy. Tape the paper pattern (if applicable) and acetate on to a cutting mat to prevent it sliding around, and start cutting out the stencil, following the lines. Use a small to medium craft knife or a scalpel with a new blade. Take extra care when cutting around corners and when cutting out the more intricate parts of the design. Remove all the cuttings and you are ready to get stencilling. You can enlarge or reduce a design on a photocopying machine. When using your stencil, there is no right or wrong side. Some designs

call for an image to be reversed – to do this, simply flip your stencil, having first made sure it is clean and dry.

If you're using the stencil motif as an embroidery outline, use a very sharp, hard pencil which will leave a fine line on the fabric, or an air-soluble pen, or a thin permanent marker. Water-based fabric paints are ideal for painting through the stencil. Some darken slightly as they dry.

Use stencil brushes to apply the paints. These have stiff, blunt-cut bristles and come in different sizes – the smaller the cutout, the smaller the brush should be.

The best fabrics for stencilling are smoothly woven, natural fabrics. It is best to wash the fabric first to test for shrinkage and colourfastness, and to remove the finish on the fabric. Suitable fabrics include cotton, cotton mixes and linen.

YOU WILL NEED

* ❋ Acetate, cutting mat, craft knife or scalpel
* ❋ Fabric, washed and ironed
* ❋ Fabric paints, including white
* ❋ Stencil brushes
* ❋ Sharp, hard (H) pencil
* ❋ Masking tape
* ❋ Lining paper
* ❋ Spatula for mixing paints (optional)
* ❋ Old white saucer
* ❋ Paper towels

Outlining a stencil design

Lay the fabric out on a flat surface and secure it with strips of masking tape. Position the stencil and hold it firmly in place with masking tape. Using a sharp H pencil, draw round the inner edges of the cutout area, keeping the line as light and fine as possible. Alternatively, use an air-soluble pen – the marks will disappear in a few days.

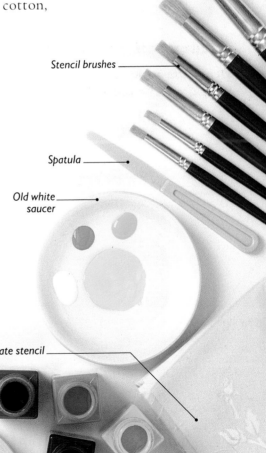

Stencil brushes

Spatula

Old white saucer

Acetate stencil

Fabric paints

Masking tape

Using the Stencils

Before you start, wash the fabric to remove any manufacturer's finishes. Cover the work surface with scrap paper or lining paper to prevent the paint staining it, then stretch the fabric taut before starting to stencil it.

Using the stencil

Stencil all the cutouts in the first colour before applying the second colour. Clean and dry the stencil and brush before applying each new colour. To avoid smudging the paint, lift the stencil off the fabric rather than sliding it off.

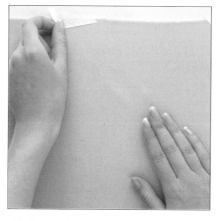

1 Cover the work surface with lining paper. Lay the fabric over the paper and smooth it out. Hold the fabric taut with strips of masking tape.

2 Use masking tape to cover all the cutout areas on the stencil you don't need for the first colour. Tape the stencil firmly in place.

3 Dip your brush in the paint and work it on the saucer until it is quite dry – avoid loading too much paint on the brush.

4 Using a firm up and down movement, dab the first colour through the cutout, starting at the outer edges and working inwards.

5 Remove the stencil and take off the masking tape. Clean and dry the stencil with water and a paper towel. If the paint is difficult to remove, scrub it gently with an old toothbrush.

Untidy outlines
Paint can seep under the edges of the stencil, blurring the outlines if the paint is too wet or there is too much paint on the brush. To avoid this, make sure the brush is fairly dry before you apply the colour.

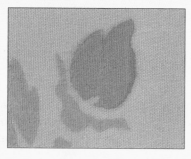

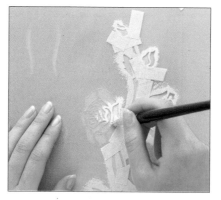

6 If any cutouts you *don't* need for the second colour butt up close to the second colour cutouts, mask them out. Leave a few areas unmasked to help you reposition the stencil, then apply the second colour as before.

7 Allow the paint to dry thoroughly. To set the colour, place a piece of kitchen paper on the paint and press it with a hot iron, according to the instructions provided by the fabric paint manufacturer.

Using Fabric Paints

Depending on how you apply the paint through the stencil – dry-brushing, stippling or sponging – you can create three completely different finishes to suit a range of embroidery stitches.

Dry brushing For a light, streaky finish which adds texture to areas which will remain unstitched, apply the paint with dry brushing.

Stippling For a background of solid colour, suitable for filling stitches such as satin stitch, use a brush to stipple on the paint.

Sponging For a speckled finish, suitable for a wide variety of stitches, apply paint with a sponge.

Materials

Brushes and sponges For dry brush and stippling, use a good quality stencil brush. For sponging, natural sponges are best. They are expensive, but you will only need a small one.

Paint palettes Art and craft shops sell ceramic and plastic palettes for mixing the paints on. Some old white saucers or small bowls cost less and will do the job just as well. Using an old brush, a flexible plastic palette knife, or a small wooden stick to mix the paints, will help avoid damaging your stencil brush, or clogging it with paint. Old teaspoons are useful for dishing out the paints from the jars.

Testing the colour

Getting the colour of the paint right is very important. The steps on page 72 explain how to do simple colour mixing, and how different fabric colours affect the paint colour. You should always test your colours and practise your techniques before starting to stencil. Use a piece of the same fabric for testing the paint colours.

Stippling the paint gives even coverage.

Dry brushing gives a lighter effect.

Sponging the paint gives a speckled finish.

Applying paint through a stencil

Stippling Use a stencil brush to apply the paint with a firm up and down movement. The paint should sink into the fabric, rather than simply coating the surface.

Dry brushing Dip the tip of the stencil brush into the paint, and dab off the excess on kitchen paper until the brush is nearly dry. Stroke it across the cutout to create a light film of colour.

Sponging Dip the sponge in the paint and squeeze it almost dry. Dab off any excess paint on a scrap of paper, then dab the paint lightly through the stencil cutout.

Making a pastel colour

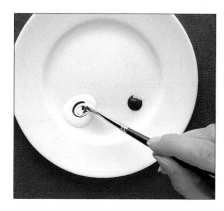  

1 Put about 1tbsp (15ml) of white paint on the saucer. Swirl in a tiny dab of the main colour.

2 Mix the colours with a small brush or a flexible palette knife, then test the colour on a spare piece of fabric.

3 Dry the paint with a hairdryer before checking the colour – the paint darkens as it dries. Add more white or coloured paint, as necessary.

Making a dark colour lighter

1 Put about 1tbsp (15ml) of the main colour on the saucer, and add in a tiny dab of white paint.

2 Mix the paint, then test the colour on a spare piece of fabric. Dry the paint as shown above.

Fabric paint colours can look very different depending on the amount of white you mix in. The fabric strips below show four different colours, each mixed with progressively larger amounts of white.

Choosing the right colour

Always test the paint colour on your fabric before starting to stencil, as the fabric colour can alter the paint colour. Colours are truest on white (above right). On mauve, for example (below right), the same colours look drab. For clearer paint colours on coloured fabrics, add a little white to the paint.

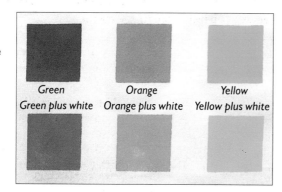

Green
Green plus white

Orange
Orange plus white

Yellow
Yellow plus white

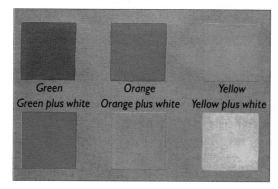

Green
Green plus white

Orange
Orange plus white

Yellow
Yellow plus white

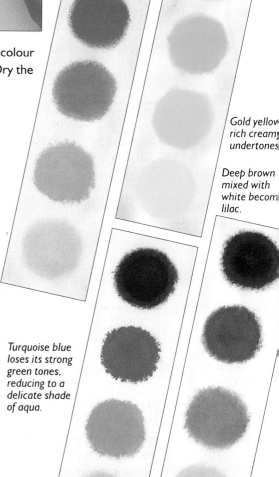

Vermilion lightens to pink.

Gold yellow rich creamy undertones

Deep brown mixed with white become lilac.

Turquoise blue loses its strong green tones, reducing to a delicate shade of aqua.

Stencilling Borders

You can use stencils to produce a whole range of borders to create colourful edgings for soft furnishings and clothing. Try splashing a family of ducklings along a towel, for example, or plant cheery sunflowers round the hem of a child's dress.

There are two main types of border, non-continuous and continuous.

Continuous borders consist of a series of interlocked motifs. You start stencilling at one edge of your fabric and keep going until you reach the opposite edge, as shown below. Flowing stencil designs, such as the sweet peas stencil, are ideal for this type of border.

Non-continuous borders consist of single motifs, usually separated by small gaps (see overleaf). You can use just one cutout, or combine two or more cutouts from the same stencil sheet. You can even mix cutouts from different stencils to create your own designs. Bold images, like elephants, sunflowers and shells, are ideal for non-continuous borders.

Making a continuous border

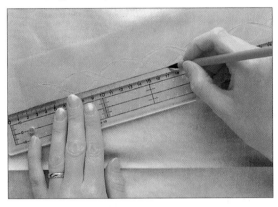

1 Decide where to position the border. Fold and press the fabric to mark the position of the lower edge of the border. You will use this foldline as a positioning guide. On the stencil sheet, use a pencil and ruler to mark the base of the motif.

2 Position the stencil at the left-hand edge of the fabric, carefully aligning the horizontal line on the stencil sheet with the foldline on the fabric. Stencil the cutout.

A continuous border uses a single cutout to create a flowing, unbroken design.

3 Move the stencil along to the right, aligning the line on the sheet with the foldline. Match up the left-hand edge of the cutout with the right-hand edge of the border section you have just stencilled. Stencil the second section of the border. Continue in this way until the border is complete.

HANDY HINT

HANDLING YOUR STENCILS
If you decide to buy intricate stencils rather than making your own, you may find that not all the cutouts have been removed. In this case, tape the stencil to a cutting board and carefully run the blade of a craft knife along the cutting line.

Making a non-continuous border

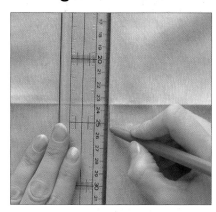
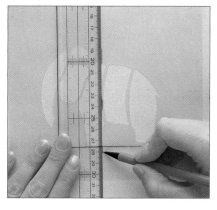
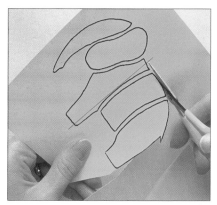

1 Fold and press the fabric to mark the position of the base of the border – use this foldline as a positioning guide. Fold the fabric in half to find the centre of the foldline. Mark this point with an air-erasable pen.

2 Using a pencil and ruler, mark a horizontal line along the base of the cutout. Then draw a vertical line through the centre of the cutout. Use these lines to position the cutouts accurately along the border.

3 Draw round the cutout on to paper or thin card and mark a vertical line through the centre. Cut out the shape to make a template to help you plan out the border.

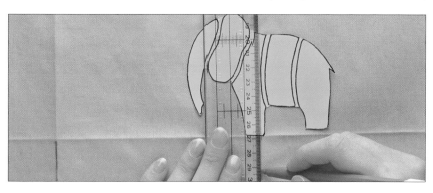

4 Working out from the centre, plan out the positions of the motifs, making sure that the gaps between them are all the same size. If you find you have incomplete motifs at the ends, reduce or enlarge the gaps. Mark the position of the centre of each motif on the horizontal foldline.

HANDY HINT

QUICK FIX

Very fine designs need to be firmly secured to the fabric to prevent paint seeping under the bridges. Spray Mount – a spray-on adhesive – ensures that all areas of the stencil adhere closely to the fabric, so the cutout is less likely to shift slightly while you are stencilling. Spray the back of the stencil with the adhesive, leave it to dry, then press it in place.

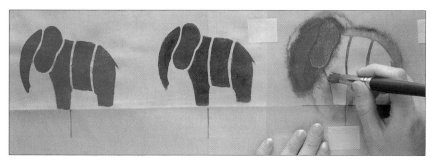

5 Position the cutout at the marked centre point, aligning the vertical and horizontal guidelines on the stencil and the fabric. Stencil the motif. Continue in this way, working out from the centre.

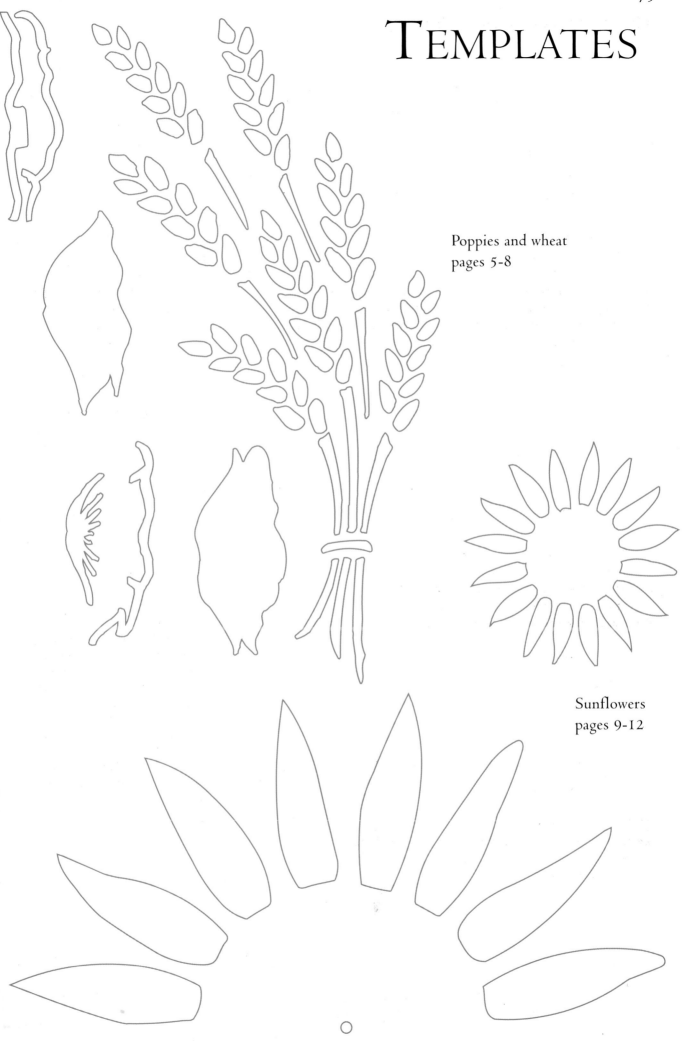

TEMPLATES

Poppies and wheat
pages 5-8

Sunflowers
pages 9-12

Sweetpeas
pages 13-18

Pear perfect
pages 19-22

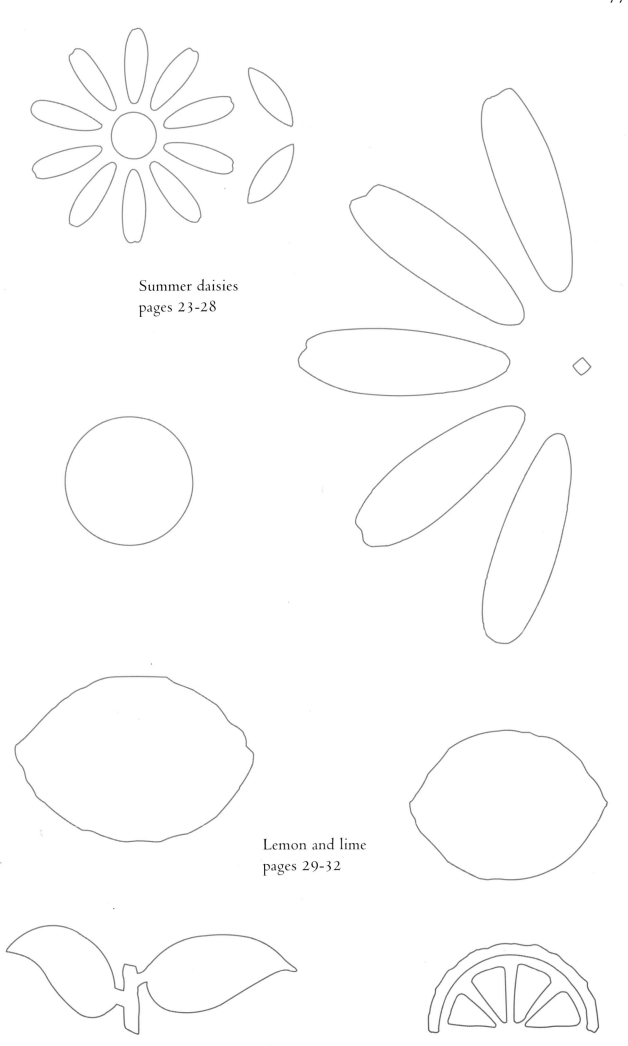

Summer daisies
pages 23-28

Lemon and lime
pages 29-32

Vases of flowers
pages 33-38

Lavender and roses
pages 43-46

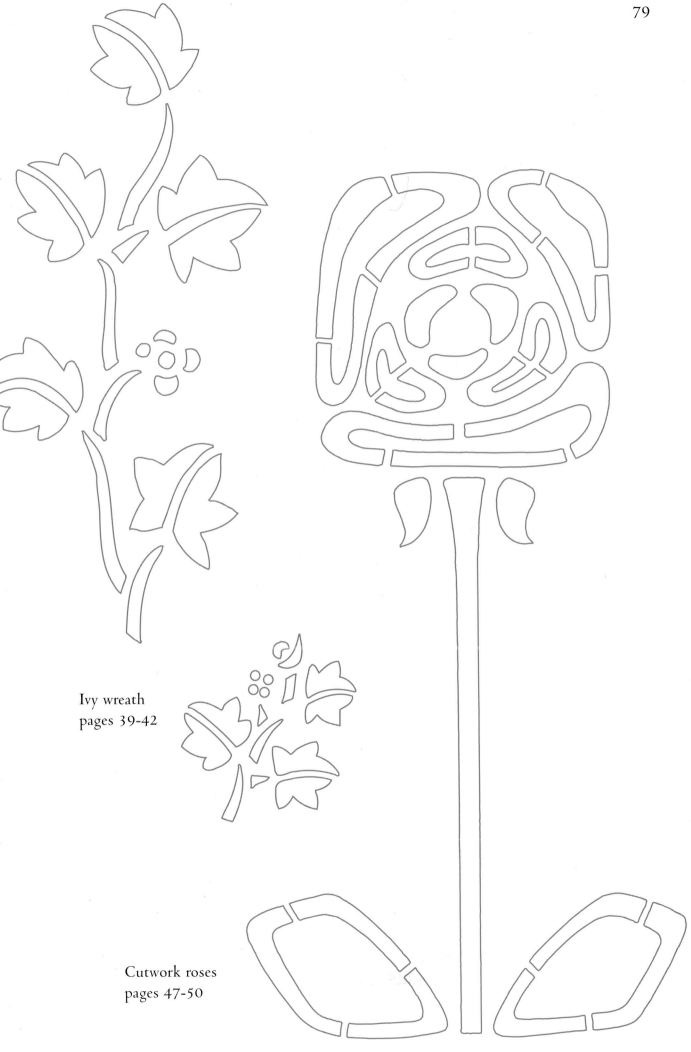

Ivy wreath
pages 39-42

Cutwork roses
pages 47-50

Bamboo trellis
pages 53-56

Gypsophila
pages 57-60